Arrival of

THE FIRST
AFRICANS

in Virginia

Arrival of
THE FIRST AFRICANS
in Virginia

— · —

RIC MURPHY

THE
History
PRESS

Published by The History Press
Charleston, SC
www.historypress.com

First published 2020

Manufactured in the United States

ISBN 9781467145985

Library of Congress Control Number: 2020931969

To the Angolans
who sailed on the San Juan Bautista
and their descendants near and far

CONTENTS

When the missionaries arrived, the Africans had the land and the missionaries had the Bible.

They taught us how to pray with our eyes closed.
When we opened them, they had the land and we had the Bible.

—Jomo Kenyatta (1891–1978)

PREFACE

The transatlantic slave trade that took place over a 360-year period, now referred to as the Middle Passage, was the largest forced deportation of people in recorded history. Over 12.5 million men, women and children were taken from Africa and transported to Europe, North America, South America and the West Indies. The cruelty of forced deportation and the inhumane conditions aboard the slave vessels included starvation, disease and severe punishment, all of which resulted in, on average, a 15 percent reduction of human cargo on each voyage. Of the 12.5 million Africans captured and deported, only 10.0 million Africans arrived at their port of call; from there, only 350,326 were brought to the English colonies in North America, later to be known as the United States.

The institution of slavery originates in the stories of ancient and biblical times. It was practiced by different cultures, nationalities and religions and was not new, unique or limited just to Africa. The Byzantine–Ottoman wars and the Ottoman wars in Europe resulted in the taking of large numbers of Christian slaves, especially among the Slavic peoples of central and eastern Europe. Slavery became common within much of Europe during the Dark Ages and continued into the Middle Ages. As its existence has been recorded from the beginning of time, the institution of slavery was socially and morally accepted by cultures all around the world, bolstered by the fact that Jesus was a slave, as evidenced by the teachings of the Bible.

Intercontinental slavery grew in the late 1400s, when European ships visited Africa's coastal trading posts in search of items to trade, including people. Africa's caste system, where villages, tribal communities and urbanized areas were divided along social status, had a ready supply of enslaved people for sale. Prisoners of war, criminals, debtors or the poor and low caste became dispensable victims of the early slave trading with the Europeans. As European colonization expanded during the 1500s, the need for inexpensive labor became the driving force behind the escalation of exporting African slaves to New World colonies.

The genesis behind the transatlantic slave trade was the European desire to find the cheapest labor pool to produce and export coffee, cotton, indigo, rice, sugar, tar and tobacco and to strip colonized countries of their precious metals. Once European nations learned how to build the mighty ships needed to navigate the treacherous conditions of the Atlantic Ocean, colonization expanded rapidly to what was referred to at the time as the "New World."

Colonial nations, governments and profiteers reaped tremendous profits from the transatlantic slave trade, fostering a belief system of intellectual and racial superiority over the conquered Africans. These beliefs were translated into governmental policies that suggested Africans were biologically, intellectually and psychosocially inferior to the Europeans and therefore were better off being enslaved. First, the European countries of Denmark, England, France, Netherlands, Portugal, Spain and Sweden sought to expand their territorial holdings beyond their national boundaries; then Brazil and the United States joined, each for national greed and military expansion.

WITH THEIR MAPS AND their compasses, European explorers found tremendous fortunes in colonization, and built larger and heavier ships to eventually carry twelve million men, women and children from Africa to trading posts all along the North and South Atlantic Ocean. A comprehensive Trans-Atlantic Slave Trade Database developed in 2018 documents all slave voyages from Africa during the period of 1514 to 1866 as part of the transatlantic slave trade. The interactive database provides information on 34,934 slave voyages and the 12.5 million enslaved people who were forced from Africa and deported around the world.[1] The database also supports Virginia's colonial records describing the events that happened in August 1619, specifically the arrival of the first documented Africans in English North America.[2]

THE ARRIVAL OF AFRICANS in North and South America was an amazing feat when one considers the circumstances in which they arrived. These men, women and children, taken from their homelands against their will, endured tremendous hardship in their journey, only to arrive in the Americas to face tremendous uncertainty. Until recently, we did not know their names or stories; each was lost to history. These forgotten people contributed individually and collectively to the success of many world economies. They descended from rich cultures, advanced societies and abundant lands teeming with precious metals, beautiful mountaintops, fertile soil and proud people.

And I am proud to be descended from them.

Although the Angolans from the *San Juan Bautista* were not the first Africans to arrive in the Americas or the first to arrive in North America, their stories, initially beyond recall, have now been well documented. Now, modern researchers and knowledge-seekers can establish particular historical events as the start of African American history. Their history, along with history of their predecessors and successors, can be found in libraries, museums and private collections all around the world. I am profoundly grateful that original source materials were available to me to conduct my research so that I could bring a different perspective on who these people were, the historical factors that made their journey so important and their descendants, who helped to make their lives so historic.

In order to avoid confusion when summarizing and analyzing historical and colonial publications, I've rewritten more outdated language to ensure ease of reading; however, every measure was taken not to change the legal meaning of any passage. If a passage or word was taken out of context, my apologies, as that was not my intent or desire.

In particular, it should be noted that in referencing John Rolfe's description of the "20 and Odd Negroes," there is an understanding and acceptance that within the past ten years, the words *negro* and *Negroes* have been deleted from a number of federal and state-issued government forms, rules and regulations. In 2013, the U.S. Census Bureau stated that it would no longer use these words and deleted them from the census forms and other surveys. The word, derivative of the Spanish and Portuguese word for black, was used to describe the indigenous people of various African nations and their descendants around the world. Several iterations of the word have been used in the most derogatory manner to describe Americans of African descent. During the colonial period, which these bodies of work cover, the word *negro* was commonly used in conversation, in written works such as letters, and in various publications, including legal documents such as the ones constantly referred to in this body of work. However, the more inflammatory usage of the word can also be found in the same documents, and most present-day readers would find these words offensive. While Americans of African descent may have referred to themselves as Negroes during the colonial period, modern Americans of African descent do not.[3]

I have also rewritten passages where the word or its derivatives were used, instead using the more acceptable modern terminology, such as *African*, *African American* or *black*, as much as possible depending on context. I have also tried, again as much as possible, to demonstrate the same respect for the usage of the term *Indigenous American*s when describing the indigenous peoples of North America.

In conducting my research and in providing source documentation, I have a profound sense of gratitude to the compilers of Virginia's colonial laws, rulings and land abstracts, including William Waller Hening,[4] Henry Read McIlwaine, Nell Marion Nugent and their respective staff and editorial teams, as authorized by the Virginia General Assembly. In order to bring veracity to the narrative, Hening's edition of *The Statutes at Large, being a Collection of all the Laws of Virginia*, is used as primary source material for documentation. Further gratitude goes to Henry Read McIlwaine (1864–1934), who served as the state librarian for the Commonwealth of Virginia and served as editor of the *Minutes of the Council and General Court of Colonial Virginia*, 1622–1632, 1670–1676, With Notes and Excerpts From Original Council and General Court Records, into 1683.

Another invaluable publication, *Cavaliers and Pioneers: Abstracts of Virginia Land Patents and Grants, 1623–1800*, by Nell Marion Nugent, provide the abstracts of the records of the colonial land office, including information on headrights. The information for each patent provides the name of the patentee; the number of acres in the patent and the county in which the land was situated at the time the patent was issued; the date of the patent, the book and page of recordation; a description of the location of the land; and, if applicable, the names of the persons on the basis of whose transportation the patent was due. The index is invaluable, for it provides the names of many of the original colonial Africans and the names and locations of properties they owned. It was used to add additional credibility to the narrative of original Africans and their descendants.

The staff of several libraries and historical archives provided a tremendous amount of time and knowledge, each contributing a unique understanding of the period and of the collections in their possessions, including the Kate

Waller Barrett Branch, Special Location Collections Branch, Alexandria Public Library (special thanks to Leslie Anderson, Tricia Walker, Greg Pierce and Mark Zoeter); the Bishop Payne Library, Virginia Theological Seminary; The Virginia Library; the Virginia Historical Society; the Boston Public Library; the Plymouth Public Library; Andrew D. Boisvert and the staff at the Daughters of the American Revolution Library; the Massachusetts Historical Society; the New England Historic Genealogical Society, the Public Broadcasting Services and the National Park Services.

For their additional guidance and historical context to the subject matter and its relationship to the period, I am deeply grateful to my advisors, including Alexis Bobrik, Robert F. Burns, Douglas A. Cornwall, Joseph D. Feaster Jr., Bill Nelson, Calvin Pearson, Kathleen Knight, Dr. Reverend Elbert Ransom, Timothy Stephens and Mario Valdes.

I would also like to thank the staffs of the Embassy of the Republic Angola and the Embassy of Japan for their historical context.

A profound thank-you.

INTRODUCTION

In 2019, Americans celebrated an important milestone in American history, the commemoration of the 400th anniversary of the first recorded Africans in English North America (present-day United States). Documented in early colonial records, these men, women and children were known as the "20 and Odd" Africans, in reference to a letter written by John Rolfe in 1620 to the Virginia Company of London.[5] After being illegally stolen from the Spanish galleon the *São João Bautista* (*San Juan Bautista*), the first documented Africans arrived on the English ship *White Lion* in the English colony of Virginia on August 25, 1619. Subsequently, the remaining kidnapped Angolans arrived on the *Treasurer* in 1620 and continued to arrive over a three-year period on other ships.[6]

The 180-ton *White Lion* initially dropped anchor and landed at Point Comfort along the body of water known as Hampton Roads (present-day Hampton, Virginia), an outlying region of the Virginia colony, before it docked and reportedly "sold" these new arrivals in exchange for victuals (food).[7] Their historic journey documents a fascinating story of international colonialism, treason, piracy, kidnapping, enslavement, the law of English headrights and colonial indentureship. This history is especially important to many African Americans today, as they may be descended from those Africans brought to the colonies between 1619 and 1700 and may even descend from at least one of these first Angolans from the *San Juan Bautista*. Connecting to real history and the story of their ancestors is an important, deeply personal journey.

As described herein in greater detail, the first documented Africans came from highly developed communities steeped in culture and tradition similar to European kingdoms of that period. Citizens of these communities were skilled in forestry, agriculture and animal husbandry. They were well educated and intelligent; many spoke multiple languages, including Spanish, Portuguese and English as well as their own tribal languages. They were baptized and learned the catechism from Catholic missionaries and priests, and each had Spanish or Portuguese Christian names reflecting their religious upbringings. The royal capital city they came from had traded for centuries with the great cities of Europe. This not only bolstered the Africans' economies but also exposed them to the communicable diseases of Europe, making them immune over generations to some of the common illnesses of the Europeans. The Africans taken to the Virginia colony brought the very skills and vigor needed for the colony to survive and thrive. In fact, as evidenced by the prolific period documents, they brought exactly the necessary skills that the European settlers lacked.

As the field of African American history has evolved over the past fifty years, the body of knowledge for the life, times and legal status of Americans of African descent during the colonial period has grown significantly. And yet, despite this heightened awareness, some scholars continue to propagate a narrative that is neither accurate nor factual and reflects old assumptions based on misconception. These narratives intentionally omit the historical importance of the first documented Africans to the very survival of the Virginia colony during the earliest days of its existence. The false narrative perpetuated by ignoring the significant contributions of these first Africans has stained American history while simultaneously denying an entire race of American citizenry the opportunity to fully understand and embrace the true history and rightful place of their ancestors in American history. This is based on the historical perception that all Africans and their descendants, enslaved or not, were an inherently inferior people as predicated in the prolific works of men such as Joseph Arthur de Gobineau (1816–1882), who, in one such work, describes the racial groupings of the world's people and the superiority of people of European and western Asian heritage. Although Gobineau's writings were not the first to draw sharp contrasts between the European and African cultures and their peoples, his modern theories on the ethnically pure "Aryan race" were noted in the nineteenth and twentieth centuries and are believed by some today.

The residual effects of Gobineau's writings and the similar beliefs of others in the seventeenth century permeate teachings, public discussions and political discourse even in modern-day America—even in the highest office of the government. On January 11, 2018, U.S. president Donald Trump, during a heated exchange with lawmakers in the White House on the topic of immigration, purportedly referred to Haiti, El Salvador and regions of Africa as "shithole countries."

According to numerous sources who attended the meeting, as reported by several news outlets, including the *Washington Post*, the president said, "Why are we having all these people from shithole countries come here?" According to the same sources, the president asked why the government wasn't doing more to recruit more people from Norway into the country. This attitude is unsurprising, as one of President Trump's primary campaign promises was to build a wall on the Mexican border. Since his election in 2016, he has taken several steps to reduce immigration from certain countries and to reduce the number of undocumented immigrants in the United States.[8]

The president's derogatory comments about Haiti, El Salvador and Africa, along with his desire to reduce immigration from nations with populations of brown and black people while celebrating immigration from predominantly white nations, echoes the narrow-minded beliefs perpetuated by Gobineau and others still today: that brown and black people are inherently inferior to white people.

While Trump's stunning and disturbing remarks received substantial national attention from the press and pundits on both sides of the political divide, these white supremacist beliefs are not substantiated by the facts. According to research conducted by the Migration Policy Institute, using federal databases found in the public domain, of the 1.4 million who are age twenty-five and older, 41 percent of Africans from sub-Saharan Africa "have a bachelor's degree, compared with 30 percent of all immigrants and 32 percent of the U.S.-born population. Of the 19,000 U.S. immigrants from Norway—a country Trump reportedly told lawmakers is a good source of immigrants—38 percent have college educations."[9] The 2017 Migration Policy Institute study on sub-Saharan immigrants further explains:

> *Sub-Saharan immigrants have much higher educational attainment compared to the overall foreign- and native-born populations. In 2015, 39 percent of sub-Saharan Africans (ages 25 and over) had a bachelor's degree or higher, compared to 29 percent of the total foreign-born population and 31 percent of the U.S.-born population. Nigerians and South Africans were the most highly educated, with 57 percent holding at least a bachelor's degree, followed by Kenyans (44 percent), Ghanaians (40 percent), Liberians (32 percent),*

and Ethiopians (29 percent). Sub-Saharan Africans participated in the labor force at a higher rate than the overall immigrant and U.S.-born populations. In 2015, about 75 percent of sub-Saharan immigrants (ages 16 and over) were in the civilian labor force, compared to 66 percent and 62 percent of the overall foreign- and native-born populations, respectively. Compared to the total foreign-born population, sub-Saharan Africans were much more likely to be employed in management, business, science, and arts occupations (38 percent) and much less likely to be employed in natural resources, construction, and maintenance occupations (3 percent). The occupational distribution by origin group follows the pattern of educational attainment: South African (62 percent) and Nigerian (53 percent) immigrants were the most likely to be in management positions, while 37 percent of Somali immigrants worked in production, transportation, and material moving occupations.[10]

Many wonder why the Angolans from the *San Juan Bautista* were so special and why their arrival in America should be treated with such deference. The short answer is that history tends to repeat itself, and the first record of Africans who arrived in 1619, much like those recorded by the 2015 Migration Policy Institute study on sub-Saharan Africans, indicates that everything American history would have us believe about these Africans contradicts the realities of American slavery and the enslaved men, women and children who were kidnapped from Africa and brought to the Americas.

To better understand the historical importance of the arrival of the Angolans in English North America, this narrative examines well-documented first-person accounts that describe how the Virginia colony was suffering economically and how its settlers were suffering from famine, disease and constant attacks from the indigenous people who had little desire to share their land with foreign intruders. These first documented Angolans brought with them unique skills that the colony badly needed.

The book was written not only to tell the story of these Angolans from the *San Juan Bautista* but also to establish their place in a true historical context and to ensure that their contributions and legacy no longer remain unknown in American history.

THEIR ARRIVAL

During the early months of 1619 in western Africa, thousands of captive Angolans were taken to the seaport village of Luanda, Angola, to be sold to foreign lands as enslaved people. Thirty-six ships awaited them in the harbor, the empty cargo holds ready to be filled with frightened men, women and children uncertain of their destiny.

Originally from Ndongo, West Africa, the royal region of Kabasa, a young man by the name of Antonio and a young woman named Maria would be forced to board a Spanish ship, the *San Juan Bautista*, intended to be sold under contract in Vera Cruz, New Spain (present-day Mexico). Some thirty-five years later, Antonio would change his name and become known as Anthony Johnson; his wife, Maria, would be known as Mary. The Johnsons, along with their sons, would come to prosper as free people of color, eventually owning nearly one thousand acres of land in English North America.

When Antonio and Mary, along with other Africans who originally were on board the *San Juan Bautista*, arrived in Virginia, the English colony was on the verge of total collapse. Not a single plantation had made the profit expected by the financial backers in London. The English inhabitants were ill-prepared to sustain themselves. Many were dying from disease, others from starvation, and a recent Indigenous American attack had killed two-thirds of the population.

The Virginia Company of London, which funded the colony in North America, sent the poor from the inner city's overcrowded slums to Virginia to work as laborers under a contractual indenture agreement. The newly indentured servants from London's ghettos had little to no agricultural skills or knowledge of animal husbandry that could aid in the development of the newly established colony. Many were victims of the harsh realities of England's clearly defined caste system. They were poorly educated, with little knowledge or training in religious education, and a disproportionate number were illiterate and often victimized by their countrymen.

When the Africans first arrived in the Virginia colony in 1619, they brought with them the skills that the colony desperately needed in order to grow and prosper. These Angolans, having descended from the spirits of their great elders, who had domesticated animals for centuries, were experienced in animal husbandry. They were farmers, and they inherently understood agricultural techniques and the importance of crop rotation in order to maximize profits. They were taught catechism by the Catholic nuns and missionaries, were able to read and write and had mathematical computation skills necessary to bargain and trade effectively. When these Africans were put to work in the Virginia colony, their value was instantly recognizable; the plantations on which they lived immediately increased their crop production and quickly began to turn profits never realized before, as evidenced by records found in the colonial registries.

The knowledge, skills and abilities of the Angolans made them unique in many ways, and the successes of Antonio and his wife, Maria (Anthony and Mary Johnson), reflect the challenges, survival and perseverance of Virginia's first documented Africans, who set sail involuntarily from Luanda, Angola. Their perseverance is echoed in the intellectual aptitude of another survivor of the *San Juan Bautista*, John Gowen, who, despite his African birth, became highly respected for his legal mind and served as an office holder in the Virginia administration by becoming a colonial magistrate for York County.[11]

While the stories of Anthony and Mary Johnson and John Gowen are not unique, they reflect the true embodiment of the American pioneering spirit during the earliest days of the colonial period. Their stories also highlight the tremendous contributions of countless Africans to the survival and success of the colonies. The Angolans from the *San Juan Bautista* were integral to building this great nation from the earliest days of its existence. This commitment to America is also seen in the determination of another *San Juan Bautista* survivor, Juan Pedro, a military hero who was executed on the battlefields of Maryland at Severn River because of his religious beliefs. Juan Pedro refused to change his Portuguese birth name and held on to his deep religious beliefs, consistent with our deeply held beliefs today regarding personal freedoms and religious tolerance.

Not only are these Angolans noteworthy simply because they contradict the perception that colonial slaves were downtrodden and inferior to the white Europeans, but many also epitomized the culture and status of the royal kingdom they called home.

Kidnapped from the majestic city of Kabasa, Ndongo, these once-royal subjects lived approximately 150 miles from the Atlantic Ocean in central West Africa in the present-day nation of Angola. As described by Portuguese explorers, these Africans were born in the capital city of Kabasa, nestled in the highlands of the Bié Plateau region.

Ndongo was once part of the great kingdom of Kongo; according to Portuguese explorer Diogo Cão, one of the first European men to "discover" the area in 1483, Kongo was one of the greatest kingdoms of Central Africa. In his writings, Cão reported that Kongo covered more than 115,000 square miles and was home to four million people. His firsthand account describes the Kingdom of Kongo as being founded much like the royal kingdoms of Europe: by consolidating power through military conquests of weaker rulers.[12]

Diogo Cão further described the Bantu people, the indigenous people of the region, as coming from some of the most influential and powerful African kingdoms in equatorial West Africa, including the kingdoms of Kongo, Ndongo, Loango and Matamba (present-day Angola and Democratic Republic of the Congo). He acknowledged that the people were "an advanced, permanently settled farming and herding people who forged iron tools and weapons, and who lived in the same towns year-round."[13]

Some two hundred years after Diogo Cão, the capital city of Kabasa, where Anthony and Mary Johnson, John Gowen and Juan Pedro came from, had progressed even further.

In 1491, when Kongo's King Nzinga learned more about the Catholic faith from the Portuguese explorers and their missionaries, he made the decision to convert to Catholicism. The king was baptized, along with six of his senior chiefs, and all took the names of prominent Portuguese noblemen in honor of their newfound religion. Upon conversion, Kongo's King Nzinga was baptized as King João I.[14]

From this point forward, it became common for Kongo's ruling class to take Spanish and Portuguese names, which helps explain why the first Africans who arrived in the Virginia colony in 1619 had familiar European names. Names such as Margarita, Isabella, Antonio, Juan and Pedro were reflective of their Christian upbringing and also names that were easy to anglicize. These Portuguese names signified the social prominence and religious education of each of the Africans in Kongolese society.[15]

The long history of diplomatic and religious exchange programs between Portugal and Kongo resulted in the children of prominent Kongolese royal families benefiting from learning abroad, especially studying the fundamentals of Christianity at the Monastery of São Eloi and elsewhere in Lisbon, Portugal. Other young men were sent to Europe to further their educational studies.[16]

At a time when the Protestant Reformation was beginning to take hold in northern Europe, Pope Leo X was extremely impressed and appreciative of the rapid conversion to Catholicism in the Kingdom of Kongo. In an expression of his appreciation, in 1518, the Pope paid one of the highest compliments to the kingdom when he named King João I's grandson Henry, the son of King Afonso, as the first bishop of black Africa.[17]

When the Portuguese first came to Africa, they brought Catholicism and the Bible, while the Africans had the people, the land and the minerals. But by 1619, once valuable mineral deposits were found in the Kabasa region of the Bié Plateau, the Africans were left with religion and the Bible, and the Portuguese, after several wars, had taken military steps to secure ownership of the people, the land and its minerals.

The region of Africa where Anthony and Mary Johnson, John Gowen and Juan Pedro originated from, near the highlands of the Bié Plateau region, was rich in valuable silver deposits, a commodity of extreme interest of the Portuguese.[18] While the larger relationship between the Portuguese and the Ndongos was amicable and mutually beneficial for over a century, the discovery of silver deposits served as a major incentive for the Portuguese to overpower and colonize the African people and to take control of the interior area from the highlands down to the Atlantic Ocean to the west.[19]

As early as 1570, the Portuguese began to establish permanent outposts along the coast of the West African kingdom and took military action to invade the land between the Atlantic and the Bié Plateau. The Portuguese soon found out that the Ndongos were a formidable force, able to repel the constantly advancing Portuguese armies. In late 1618 and early 1619, the Portuguese army—with guns, cannons and African mercenaries supplementing the European military forces—was finally able to overpower the inhabitants in the royal capital city. Over a two-year period, more than fifty thousand Angolans were captured and sold into slavery.[20]

The first wave of over two thousand captured Ndongos came from the royal city of Kabasa.[21] They were processed and forced to march over 150 miles to the slave pens on the coastline, where over thirty-six slave ships, having arrived over a period of months, waited for them. As they were being processed in the Portuguese seaport of São Paulo de Loanda (also known as Luanda), Captain Manuel Mendes de Acuña (also known as Cunha) of the Japanese-built Spanish ship *San Juan Bautista* was processing his own paperwork.[22] Captain de Acuña was under contract to Antonio Fernandes Delvas to deliver his shipment of enslaved men, women and children to Vera Cruz, New Spain (present-day Mexico).[23]

Once de Acuña made all the contractual arrangements, he was ready to receive his shipment and depart on a journey that would take three to four months or more, depending on the weather. The slavers at the slave pen selected the cargo for the *San Juan Bautista*. Each man, woman and child was carefully inspected to ensure that he or she was healthy and had enough body weight to make the long sea voyage. Chained, then branded as slaves, they were led from the slave pen and rowed out past a sand bar where they were forced on board the anchored ships. As the kidnapped people approached the slave ship, one can only imagine that the vessel appeared to grow larger and more intimidating with every step. While many protested getting on board, they were kept moving by the aggressive dock agents, who were experienced in matters such as these.

In the customary fashion, the men boarded first. Once on board, they were forced to climb down a ladder into the cargo hold. Their eyes adjusted to the darkness of the space as their noses were assaulted by the pungent air below deck. Each man was required to crouch or lie down in a tightly packed area and then secured by leg irons. The women and children were separated from the men, but their quarters also limited movement. Once at sea, this separation of the women and children from the men facilitated easy access for the crew, who often perpetuated sexual abuse and violence without fear of retaliation from the men chained below.

The crew members of the slave ship reflected the dregs of their own societies, a direct contrast to the educated, capable, enslaved Africans. The men of the crew spoke Portuguese, Spanish, English and the pidgin Kimbundu dialect of the dreaded mixed Afro-Portuguese *pomberios*, who physically escorted the kidnapped Ndongos from their homes in Kabasa in the slave cartels down to the slave pens in Luanda.

The Ndongos knew that the sailors were a hardened crew, as evidenced by their deep scars, missing limbs and overall coarse appearance. Any thoughts the kidnapped Africans may have had about rebelling had to be carefully planned. When the anchor was raised and they left the waters of the port of São Paulo, each of the 350 captives realized that they would never see Ndongo or their families again and that their lives were about to change forever.[24]

It is presumed that none of the enslaved had been on a vessel of this magnitude before, and to them, the *San Juan Bautista* was a ship from hell. As the hours turned into days and days into weeks, the conditions on board the ship became more intolerable and the air reeked of urine, feces and death.

For the men below deck, their black skin was raw, and their flesh was pink from the shackles that rubbed against their legs and feet. The wails of human suffering all around them rang in their ears, constantly reminding them of their horrific conditions. These tormented slaves had been the sons and daughters of royals and merchants, and now, week after week, they endured some of the most horrendous conditions imaginable. Shackled to one another, they were forced to lie in their own urine, feces, vomit and blood, which mingled with the waste and bodily fluids of others with whom they were shackled.

The kidnapped Africans suffered from pain and seasickness, and each day and night on the long, arduous ocean journey only weakened them further. For the men in particular, the stagnant and putrid air in the cargo hold made it hard to breathe, and the only living things that seemed to thrive aboard ship were the rats that constantly ran among the hostages and feasted on their waste. The conditions on early seventeenth-century slave ships were primitive at best, and although slavers improved conditions during the mid-seventeenth century in an attempt to have a greater financial gain by delivering healthy enslaved, the conditions on board remained rancid.

These unsanitary conditions bred debilitating and contagious diseases such as dysentery, smallpox, scurvy, measles, malaria and yellow fever. Disease was endemic, also transmitted by the rodents that were known carriers of disease and pestilence; their droppings contaminated the food that the enslaved ate. The captives' raw skin and open sores were perfect hosts for infected fleas, mites, lice and ticks that lived on the rodents. The Angolans were also sickened by the air, thick with the scent of evaporating human and vermin waste. The stench from the cargo hold and disease often created the perfect environment for many captives to commit suicide.

Several times a week, when the stench below deck became too overwhelming for the crew, the enslaved were allowed topside while the crew gathered the dead to be thrown overboard. So many of the ship's dead were thrown overboard that the *San Juan Bautista* records describe being followed by schools of sharks taking turns at the floating carcasses.

After the ship's dead were thrown overboard, the crew would throw buckets of seawater on the captives to wash the dried excrement from their bodies. The seawater would also help heal their open sores. Then, several crewmen went below deck to the belly of the ship to flush away weeks of dried human waste.

Well into their voyage at sea, nearly all of the captives on board the Spanish galleon were severely ill, and the ship's captain, Manuel Mendez de Acuña, was fearful that he would fail to deliver his human cargo to Vera Cruz. Captain Acuña recorded

> that he "has many sick aboard, and many already died." Before the frigate crossed the Atlantic and reached the West Indies a few weeks later, more than one hundred on the Bautista had died of sickness. And Vera Cruz, her intended destination, was still nearly one thousand miles away. Fearing the entire shipment would be dead before reaching Mexico, Captain Acuña paused briefly in the Caribbean for medicine and supplies that he paid for with twenty-four "slave boys he was forced to sell in Jamaica where he had to refresh."[25]

Acuña decided to redirect his ship and stopped in Jamaica, hoping to thoroughly clean his ship, restore his captives' health and deliver as much of his human cargo to Vera Cruz as possible.[26] Once he arrived in Jamaica, Acuña was able to give his captives fresh food and water. They were brought on deck in midmorning, where they were exposed to the island's fresh air and had their wounds tended. While on deck, they were forced to strengthen themselves through daily exercises. Acuña's cargo began to recover. However, although the stop in Jamaica had restored the Africans' health, it proved costly for the ship's captain. Without the proper exchange of currency, Acuña had to trade twenty-four young African boys in exchange for the food and medicine necessary for his captives. Once the ship's belly had been cleaned and sanitized with sea water, with his captives fed and a little stronger, Captain Acuña set sail for his destination of Vera Cruz.

Having left Jamaica in early July, the slave ship entered the Gulf of Mexico between Cuba and the tip of the Yucatán Peninsula. On July 15, less than five hundred miles from Vera Cruz, Acuña, while gazing at a massive band of low, ominous clouds coming in from the east, noticed that he was being stalked by two pirate ships.[27]

Having spotted the *San Juan Bautista* and hoping the galleon carried gold and silver, two converted English man-of-war ships, the *White Lion*, flying under a Dutch flag, and the *Treasurer*, sailing with a Duke of Savoy (Charles Emmanuel I of Italy) marque, gave chase, trapping the Portuguese ship *San Juan Bautista* in the Bay of Campeche.[28]

The slow-moving galleon was not designed to compete with the sleeker English pirate ships. The Africans below deck realized that something was wrong as the galleon tried to outrun its pursuers, and they could hear the commotion above deck as the crew manned their battle stations and got their cannons in position.

The slaver increased speed in an attempt to flee the pirate ships, and the galleon shook violently as the wooden timbers in the hull strained against the increasing speed. The shackled men in the cargo, unaware of what was happening above deck, likely feared that at any minute the ship would come apart and they would all drown, still helplessly chained together.

The frightened African slaves pulled hard on their shackles, hoping that the ship's vibrations would set them free. If not, they would surely drown. Instead, the jostling of the ship's speed and cannon fire flung the slaves into the air, and their shackles yanked them cruelly back down. They were tossed around violently, echoing the way the *San Juan Bautista* was being tossed into the air by cannon fire before it plunged back down against the ocean waves.

For nearly two hours, the frightened and helpless captives endured the constant cannon fire from the *White Lion* and the *Treasurer* pirate ships. Then, without warning, it all stopped.

Captain Acuña was forced to surrender his ship. In examining the aftermath, the crew found the *San Juan Bautista* was badly damaged, as was the *Treasurer*. As the pirate ships approached the starboard and port sides of the galleon, the pirates were met with the rancid stench from the cargo hold. Once the English pirates boarded the *San Juan Bautista*, they were disappointed to learn from Acuña that instead of a stash of gold and silver treasure, they had won a cargo of enslaved Africans being shipped from São Paulo de Loanda, Angola, to Vera Cruz, Mexico.[29] Hoping to make money off their human cargo, the two pirate ships conspired to take their captives and sell them to the highest bidders in either the English colony of Virginia or Bermuda.

From the cargo hold, unaware of the conversations taking place on deck, the Angolans only knew that the *San Juan Bautista* was not moving. It is presumed that the initial silence in the cargo hold was occasionally broken by a slight whisper from one of the Angolans speculating as to what was going on above deck. The Africans, still shackled in the cargo hold, were figuratively and literally in the dark. Finally, the hatch door was opened, and light poured into the hull as several men stepped down the stairs. These men had scarves wrapped around the lower portion of their faces to repel the stench and were completely unrecognizable to the Africans. Two Englishmen had their pistols drawn and likely hid daggers in their clothing. These men had lost the lottery and were forced to go down into the cargo hold to see if they could find any valuables hidden among the enslaved.

At some point, the two captains of the English pirate ships realized and finally confirmed that there was no gold to claim. The most the Englishmen could hope for was to be able to sell the Africans. The pirates decided to take the healthiest Africans on their ships and let the *San Juan Bautista* go; after the attack and extensive cannon fire, it was barely seaworthy. Sixty of the African slaves were divided between the two captains and sent to the cargo holds of the *White Lion* and the *Treasurer* for transport to either Bermuda or the English colony of Virginia.

For the second time since leaving São Paulo de Loanda, the Angolans were divided from the original 350 captives held on board the *San Juan Bautista*. The captains of the two English ships, with their foreign marques, decided to sail to the colony of Virginia, a refuge for the illegal activity of English privateers raiding Spanish ships in the Atlantic Ocean. The captains hoped that since each ship had suffered different degrees of damage from the attack on *San Juan Bautista*, they would be able to repair their ships and sell or trade the Africans for much-needed food.

While only the *Treasurer* was secretly and illegally retrofitted in Virginia as a man-of-war, neither ship was intended to be a slaver. The physical conditions of the two ships' cargo holds were slightly better than being in the cramped, disease-ridden quarters of the *San Juan Bautista*. But food was scarce for the crew, and little was available to be shared with the enslaved. The *Treasurer*, badly damaged and taking on water, became separated from the *White Lion* at some point while en route to the Virginia colony.[30]

The severely damaged *San Juan Bautista* never reached Vera Cruz. Its cargo of only 147 of the original 350 Angolans who boarded at Luanda, Angola, during the early months of 1619 would make it to their final destination in late August after being transferred at sea to the *Santa Ana*. One crucial source, a financial accounting ledger that documents these events, is found in the Spanish archives. The ledger chronicles the purchase of the original 350 enslaved in Angola, the events at sea and the delivery, receipt and sale of the remaining captives in Vera Cruz, New Spain (present-day Mexico), on August 30, 1619. According to the financial ledger:

> *Enter on the credit side the receipt of 8,657.875 pesos by Manuel Mendez de Acuña, master of the Ship* San Juan Bautista, *on 147 slave pieces brought by him into the aid port on August 30, 1619, aboard the frigate* Santa Ana, *master Rodrigo Escobar. On the voyage inbound, Mendez de Acuña was robbed at sea off the coast of Campeche by English (war ships). Out of 350 slaves, large and small, he loaded in said* Loanda *(200 under a license issued to him in Sevilla and the rest to be declared later) the English corsairs left him with only 147, including 24 slave boys he was forced to sell in Jamaica, where he had to refresh, for he had many sick aboard, and many had already died.*[31]

The transfer of the sixty or so enslaved between the *San Juan Bautista* and the two English ships in many ways benefited the enslaved Ndongos. The two English ships were relatively clean and disease-free compared to the *São João Bautista* and didn't reek of human waste and sickness. Although probably still in chains, the captives were provided more space to spread out among the barrels and crates used for storage and trade in the cargo hold, and their eventual treatment upon reaching Virginia would be very different than those who would eventually arrive in New Spain and points forward.

On August 25, 1619, the *White Lion*, captained by John Colyn Jope, was the first of the two ships to arrive at Cape Comfort (to be later called Point Comfort), where Jope reportedly sold Angolans from the *San Juan Bautista* in exchange for food. These were the first Africans to enter the Virginia colony. Four days later, the *Treasurer* arrived with additional Africans, but none on this voyage was documented as having left the ship, with the exception of an Angolan woman identified as Angelo.[32]

According to the financial ledgers, on August 30, 1619, Manuel Mendes de Acuña, captain of the *San Juan Bautista*, finally arrived in Vera Cruz, New Spain, with only 147 enslaved Africans. Of the thirty-six slave ships that arrived in Mexico, the "*San Juan Bautista* was the only slave ship among [those] arriving at Vera Cruz between 1618 and 1622 to be attacked, inbound from Angola."[33] Based on the ship's registries found in the Spanish archives from the same period, only six slave ships arrived at Vera Cruz, Mexico, each having loaded its human cargo in São Paulo de Loanda, Angola.

When Captain Jope and the *White Lion* arrived in the Virginia colony, the ship, with its crew and African captives, first arrived at the colonial outpost at Point Comfort (present-day city of Hampton). The peninsula sits between the mouths of the James and York Rivers in the body of water that stretches between the two rivers known as Hampton Roads.[34] Presumably to show proof of the African captives on board, Jope took several to the harbormaster, Commander William Tucker, expressing desire to sell or trade them.

It was at this point that three critical events took place, each having a profound and lasting impact on the immediate status and conditions of the Africans on board the *White Lion* and those to soon follow on the *Treasurer*.

First, Captain Jope was made aware that a new governor had been appointed by the Virginia Company of London to supervise the colony and that one of his charges was to stop the practice of privateering. At this point, Jope would have provided his Dutch letter of marque explaining why he was flying a foreign flag on his ship. Once his documentation was validated, in accordance to international laws, he was allowed to attack the Spanish *San Juan Bautista* and seize its property since the Dutch were still at war with Spain. After this was clarified, Jope was granted permission to visit with the settlement's leaders in Jamestown while the *White Lion* docked off Point Comfort for repairs and restocking.

Second, as Jope explained his Dutch marque, he would have likely explained his exploits with his cohort, Captain Daniel Elfrith of the *Treasurer*. It was at this time that Jope was probably made aware of the legal peril of Captain Elfrith and the demand to seize the *Treasurer* if it arrived in the colony, particularly since it was flying under the flag of the Duke of Savoy (Rivoli, Italy). The duchy had now made peace with Spain, and Elfrith's act of piracy against the Spanish *San Juan Bautista* was now considered an illegal act under international law. Therefore, Captain Elfrith and the owner(s) of the *Treasurer* had no legal claim over any items seized from the Portuguese slave ship. Further, the harbormaster probably shared that the new governor, George Yeardley, was given specific instructions to seize the *Treasurer* and arrest its captain once he arrived, as officials in London suspected that the *Treasurer* and its owners were violating international law and privateering Spanish vessels. If Elfrith was captured and proven guilty of these high crimes against international law, the penalty in London was hanging or decapitation.

Third, twenty-nine Angolans who were on the *Treasurer*, having been illegally seized in violation of international law, would be taken to the English colony on the island of Bermuda. Some of the twenty-nine would eventually and permanently return to Virginia in different phases and on different ships over several years and then dispersed throughout the colony. They left Angola as enslaved people, and had they reached Vera Cruz, New Spain, they certainly would have been sold as slaves. Given the international furor caused by their illegal seizure in the Bay of Campeche, the fate of these particular Africans would not be slavery, as previously thought, based on evidence in colonial documents recorded some fifteen to twenty years later.

After the *White Lion* was given permission to anchor, Captain Jope tried to sell the Africans he had on board for supplies. The captured Angolans from the *San Juan Bautista* were washed down and chained to one another in groups. They then disembarked on the port side of the ship and climbed down the rope ladders into several small rowboats that took them to shore. Once ashore, the Africans likely tried to determine where they were, and as the white men spoke to one another, the enslaved Angolans noticed these men were speaking in English, just as they did in Jamaica and on the ship. Perhaps a chorus of whispers arose when several of the Africans realized they were not in the Portuguese colony of Brazil or in New Spain, but probably in the land of the Englishmen, or in one of the English colonies that they had heard about back in Ndongo.

Now aware of the events in London, where King James I (son of Mary, Queen of Scotland)[35] and officers of the Virginia Company in London had taken specific steps to stamp out the rise of privateering in the Virginia colony, Captain Jope traded twenty-nine or thirty Africans he originally had on board for nothing more than some provisions for his crew.[36]

From the Africans' perspective, based on the deference given, several of the white men appeared to be in charge. Having seen or participated in the slave markets back in their home city of Kabasa, the Angolans knew how this would end based on their own firsthand experience. The wealthiest and most powerful of the men would be given the first opportunity to bid for each of them until the highest bid was recorded. However, the slave auction did not go as the Angolans expected. Although they could not hear or totally understand the English conversation, it was clear that the participants were agitated by or at least concerned about the presence of the Africans.

After the white men had a long conversation, the Africans were divided between two influential men, Governor George Yeardley of the Flowerdew Hundred Plantation and his cape merchant Abraham Piersey. The two men "bought" the Africans by providing Captain Jope and his crew with various necessities.[37] The Africans were immediately sent to work on the tobacco plantations of Yeardley and Piersey at the settlement of Fleur de Hundred.[38] While Jope was still in Jamestown, three or four days later, the second pirate ship in the consort, the *Treasurer*, arrived at Old Point Comfort.[39]

The harbormaster, Commander William Tucker, was a friend of the *Treasurer*'s owner, the powerful and well-connected Sir Robert Rich, the Earl of Warwick. Commander Tucker was well aware of the warrant out for the captain's arrest, as well as the writ to seize the *Treasurer* upon its arrival at Point Comfort. Knowing that he could provide temporary cover, Commander Tucker sent a man to Governor Yeardley asking permission for the *Treasurer* to proceed upriver.

Governor Yeardley sent three of his close advisors—Captain William Ewen, John Rolfe and his father-in-law, Captain William Pierce—to meet the *Treasurer*. However, when they arrived, the *Treasurer* was sailing off with its cargo of Africans still on board.[40] The mysterious departure of the badly damaged *Treasurer* from the colony, without unloading all of its human cargo, was just one piece of a complex puzzle cloaked in international treason, espionage, piracy and kidnapping.

Within weeks, the damaged *Treasurer*, owned by the Earl of Warwick and captained by Daniel Elfrith, sailed into the port of the Caribbean island of Bermuda. Its arrival only continued the international crisis, contributing a well-documented chronology of the first recorded Africans in English North America, and provided a wealth of information and data for present-day Americans of African descent to know the true narrative of their ancestors.

While some of the kidnapped Angolans were deposited in Bermuda, those from the *White Lion* and those who returned subsequently in the later months assisted in helping to save the Virginia colony from total financial collapse.

The Angolans from the *San Juan Bautista* who were left behind by the *White Lion* were sent farther upriver to Governor Yeardley and cape merchant Piersey's plantations. While historians have disagreed, it does not appear that there is any credible evidence that any of the other plantation owners had any other Africans residing on their plantations prior to the arrival of the Angolans from the *San Juan Bautista*.

The unique skills brought to the Yeardley and Piersey plantations by the Angolans were immediately realized. Much like the other plantations of this period, neither Yeardley's nor Piersey's plantations had realized a profit. The Virginia colony had thus far been a financial failure, and the lack of any kind of profit was a major concern for the investors. However, once the Africans arrived on these two plantations, Yeardley's and Piersey's fortunes changed dramatically.

Although the Virginia colony did not reflect seventeenth-century London, it also did not resemble the thriving trading center of Kabasa, Angola. When the Angolans from the *San Juan Bautista* arrived in Virginia, they found a primitive settlement, very different from the developed lands that they were forced to leave behind in Ndongo. Upon their arrival, historian Tim Hashaw suggested,

> *If the first Africans were amazed or intimidated upon arriving in [Virginia] in 1619, it was most likely their reaction to the primitive condition of the colony and not to English technology or culture. From day one, Jamestown's location on a sluggish stretch of the James River posed vexing problems. The water carried disease, and from 1609 to 1612 Tidewater Virginia entered a cyclical drought. Hundreds died at the Jamestown settlement in those three years, more from sickness and starvation than from Algonquian arrows.*[41]

The conditions of the colony lacked many of the support systems found in England that would have aided the settlers, and its population was still suffering from the effects of the period known as the "starving time," which only sixty out of the five hundred colonists had survived. The survivors of the Jamestown fort were forced to resort to the unthinkable—cannibalism. At any given point, life along the James River was difficult, and the English often lived within the perils of conflict with their Indigenous American neighbors. The English were primarily urbanites, unaccustomed to the demands of agriculture.

The colony of Virginia was initially a company-owned colony, founded in 1607 by the Virginia Company of London, England. In order to survive and prosper, the Virginia Company needed to constantly repopulate the colony with new laborers who helped to generate investor profits based on their hard labor. It is from these company-laborer indentured contracts and records that we find stark differences between the knowledge and skills of the newly arrived Africans compared to the overwhelming number of Englishmen who were already in the colony.

From the very beginning, the colony was a failure.[42] Although the Virginia Company had changed its governance model several times before the arrival of the Africans, its business model was fundamentally flawed. The company populated the colony with the men who had the wrong skills and training. Approximately 20 percent of the men sent were of the noble class, and as investors, they had little knowledge or understanding of how to turn the vast woodlands of the Americas into a profitable agricultural-based economy. Their intent was to find gold, silver and other precious metals and return to England as very rich men. They were not adept at living in the harsh realities of a primitive frontier life.

The other 70 to 75 percent of the men initially sent to Virginia came from the peasant class. They came primarily from the poor, overpopulated sections of London's underclass. Some of the adult men were previously homeless, prisoners who were promised commuted sentences or the financially destitute hoping for a new beginning. Many of the younger ones were merely orphans or vagrants found on the streets of London. The men and boys who came were predominantly from an urban environment and lacked the survival skills necessary to construct shelter, forage for food and survive the harsh elements of their new rural surroundings. Familiar with living in the urban squalor of the London inner city, these men for the most part were unskilled workers, devoid of any knowledge about how to carve out an existence in the wildernesses.

The ultimate failure of the colony forced the administrators of the Virginia Company back in London to constantly deploy a number of management reforms to attract and recruit laborers to the colony and to convince additional investors to infuse much-needed funds to run and support the colony. The Virginia Company's need to recruit desired workers to the colony under deplorable conditions established and expanded the institution of indentured contracts, in which workers were provided transportation to the colony with the understanding that they would work under contract for approximately seven years. After their service, these workers would be set free from their contract and hopefully be able to benefit from purchasing their own land through the headright system.

The headright system was instituted in 1618, a year before the arrival of the Angolans from the *San Juan Bautista*, as a recruitment vehicle to lure more English migrants to Virginia as laborers. Any investor of the Virginia Company of London—in other words, the owners of the Virginia colony along with residents of the colony who paid their own passage or the passage of any migrant to the colony—received fifty acres of land. The newly arrived migrants, as indentured servants, were contracted to work on investors' lands usually for about seven years and then were set free.

The chief proponent of the headright system was Sir Edwin Sandys, the treasurer of the Virginia Company of London, and one of the "ablest parliamentarians of seventeenth century England."[43] Sandys, in the role of chief executive officer, was responsible for ensuring profits for the investors of the company and for the overall management of the colony. His mission was to build and expand a permanent English colony in America for the transatlantic trade of English goods and to generate profits for the company and its investors. In his attempt to address the obstacles faced by the migrants and colonists, Sandys had his own detractors, and he was biased in his actions and decisions.

One of Sandys's major detractors was Sir Robert Rich, the Earl of Warwick, whose family's wealth enabled him to be one of the main investors in the Virginia Company. The earl also owned a vast shipping empire that included the *Treasurer*. It was Sandys who ordered the arrest of the *Treasurer*'s Captain Elfrith and the seizure of the Earl of Warwick's *Treasurer* upon its arrival up the James River in Jamestown, the hub of the colony's business and now political center.

Once Sandys learned that the *Treasurer* and its captain had escaped arrest and seizure and was now docked in Bermuda due to the acquaintance between the Earl of Warwick and harbormaster Commander Tucker, he sent investigators to Bermuda to interrogate all parties with knowledge of the events that led up to the attack on the Spanish *San Juan Bautista* and the kidnapping of its cargo of Africans on board. This interrogation included the *Treasurer*'s crew members and the Africans, who were now distributed to several plantations in Bermuda.

Sir Robert Rich, the Earl of Warwick, was deeply concerned as to his potential risk of being accused of acts of piracy against Spain by having his captain and his ship attack the *San Juan Bautista* and confiscating the Angolans, a direct violation of international law. If the accusations were proven, he would certainly be charged with treason. In order to prevent the Angolans from testifying, the Earl of Warwick sent word to Bermuda's Governor Nathaniel Butler that the Angolans needed to be separated and dispersed. The Earl of Warwick had little concern for the Angolans who arrived on the *White Lion*; after all, that ship had a legitimate Dutch marque and so had not technically committed theft. It was the Angolans who arrived on the island from the *Treasurer*, the ship that he owned with an invalid letter of marque, that concerned Sir Robert Rich. Plans were made to send some of the Africans back to Virginia and disperse them among his allies, while the earl himself would bring the "chattier" ones to his estate to keep a watchful eye on them. The remainder who arrived on the *Treasurer* were integrated and placed on area plantations on the island of Bermuda. To make sure that Governor Butler executed his instructions carefully, Sir Robert Rich gifted him two Angolans of his choosing to make sure there were no problems.

It is presumed that the Angolans who were multilingual and had some knowledge of English or Spanish—and therefore would be the most conversant and potentially damaging in an interrogation—were sent to the Earl of Warwick's spacious manor in England at Leighs Priory in Felsted, Essex, on board the *James* out of Bermuda. Four Angolans—Juan Pedro, Antonio (Anthony Johnson), Maria (Mary Johnson) and a young boy named Juan (John Gowen)—were eventually sent back to Virginia to work on the remote plantations of his business associates and confidants.

At this point, after suffering severe damage to the integrity of its hull, the *Treasurer* was a compromised, barely seaworthy vessel and remained in Bermuda. Some historians have assumed that despite its damage, the *Treasurer* left Bermuda in February 1620 and successfully arrived back in Virginia with fourteen or so Angolans.[44] While it does appear that other *San Juan Bautista* Angolans arrived in the Virginia colony, it is more likely that they came on a much smaller pinnace ordered by Bermuda's Governor Nathaniel Butler, or directly from England. Upon their arrival, the additional Angolans from the earl's *Treasurer* were dispersed and placed on the plantations of some of the most powerful men in the colony, as instructed. These men were friendly to the Earl of Warwick, and they included Captain William Pierce, Richard Kingsmill, Captain Samuel Matthew, Captain William Tucker, Captain Edward Bennett, Captain Francis West and Captain William Ewen.[45]

Unlike their kinsmen who also were forced on board the *San Juan Bautista* that fateful day in São Paulo, Luanda, Angola, and eventually deposited in the Caribbean islands of Bermuda and Jamaica, the Spanish-Portuguese ports of Vera Cruz or the sugar plantations of Brazil, these Angolans, new to the Virginia colony, were unsure of their legal status. Although for their kinsmen there was no question that their fate was to serve a perpetual life of bondage as enslaved people, for the Angolans from the *San Juan Bautista* who arrived in Virginia between 1619 and 1625, their legal status as slaves or indentured servants was an unsettled matter. Their seizure from the *San Juan Bautista* violated international law, and thus the captains and owners of the *White Lion* and the *Treasurer* had no legal claim to sell them as seized property. More importantly, based on the insurmountable evidence, Sir Robert Rich, the Earl of Warwick, took every possible measure to distance himself from the Africans rather than try to sell them and profit from their sale.

The condition of indentured servitude, a condition in which an overwhelming number of the European laborers in the Virginia colony found themselves, was not much different from the condition of the newly arrived Africans. They were all equally bought and sold for the good of the Virginia Company. Laborers, white and black, had masters who administered work assignments as well as punishments and regulated all aspects of daily living. As with the Africans, when European indentures arrived, they were sent to remote farms, plantations or outposts to clear the woodlands.

Three years after the arrival of the Angolans, the colony suffered a major setback. Although the colony had begun to thrive as a result of the growth of the tobacco crop, the very nature of its growing cycle forced further expansion of land development. Every two years, the crop depleted the soil, and as it became the predominant cash crop for the colony, expansion was required to meet the growing demand. With the emergence of the headright system and a steady stream of new immigrants entering the colony, the land grab into Indigenous American territory slowly took hold, fifty acres at a time.

According to Jamestown historian Carl Bridenbaugh, the shooting of an Indigenous American warrior provoked the Powhatan tribal council into declaring an "all-out attack against the white peril":

> On March 22, 1622, the sky did fall. Everywhere in the colony, the Native Americans attacked the Europeans and butchered 347 men, women and children, including even those of the English who had treated them fairly and well.... The plan called for the extermination of all of them...had not Governor Wyatt not been warned, thereby saving the lives of the inhabitants of Jamestown and nearby plantations.[46]

Entire plantations on the northern side of the James River were decimated or severely damaged. Whole family units were slaughtered, men, women and children; those not killed were taken back to warrior campsites. Settlers able to escape the carnage fled to the safety of Jamestown. Known as the Powhatan's Massacre of 1622, the Indigenous American slaughter had a dramatic effect on the European and African populations in the colony, resulting in dramatic changes going forward.

During this brief period of colonial history, the only documented difference between the white and black indentured servants, other than origins of birth, was the manner in which they were recorded six months later in the March 1619 and 1620 colony muster, or census. The colony's census listed a population of 885 English and other Christians in the colony and a total of 4 Indigenous Americans and 32 Africans.[47]

Prior to the attack, a few Africans who traded with local natives as representatives of the colony's settlers had developed a sense of mutual understanding. Perhaps this close contact with the natives partly explains why the Africans survived the Powhatan's massacre unscathed. However, it was also true that many Indigenous Americans regarded black-skinned people with awe, considering them to be spirits, and chose not to attack them.[48]

EUROPEAN EXPLORATION
AND THE BANTU EMPIRES

To better understand the historical importance of the arrival of the first documented Angolans from the *San Juan Bautista* in English North America, one must understand the importance of European exploration and its impact on Africa, the arrival of Europeans in North and South America and the overall effect of European colonization on the indigenous populations of the three continents.

The population of America's indigenous people, commonly called Native Americans, grew from a few thousand inhabitants to approximately twenty million people across the vast fertile lands of North and South America. In 1492, the year in which Christopher Columbus mistakenly believed he had "discovered" America, there were eight distinct indigenous nations.

After his maiden voyage in 1492, Christopher Columbus, on his second voyage in 1493, brought with him more than 1,200 men from Spain, who were scattered throughout what was referred to as the West Indies. In order to survive, the Spaniards needed inexpensive labor for menial tasks, which included culling the forest to construct settlements, clearing areas to plant the fields and eventually harvesting the crops. It was only a matter of time before the indigenous men were taken as slaves; the women were overpowered; and the valuable metals, minerals and other natural resources of the islands confiscated in the name of Spanish exploration. In short order, the indigenous people began to suffer from the aggressive pursuit of valuable commodities that were subsequently sold in Spanish markets in Europe and traded for goods in Asia.

Due to Spanish colonization, many native people died on the West Indian islands, resulting in the introduction of native enslavement from neighboring islands and, eventually, from the mainland. Indigenous Americans began to hide from the Spanish explorers and slaveholders. Those who did not hide often died from the new diseases brought by the Europeans or from the brutal treatment under the hands of their oppressors.

Native populations across all of the West Indian islands rapidly diminished in a short period of time. The large number of deaths led to the rapid decline in the availability of slave labor. That decline, combined with the Europeans' growing need for cheap workers, led to the introduction of slave labor from Africa. In 1498, on his third voyage, Columbus, having stopped at the Canary and Cape Verde Islands, began to import Africans to the West Indies, resulting in the creation of the transatlantic slave trade and driving the demand for African enslaved to an unprecedented level.

The initial introduction of African labor proved to be beneficial to the Europeans, particularly because the African enslaved could work in the tropical heat of the Caribbean islands for long, backbreaking hours, and they had immunities to European diseases. African slave labor provided a quick remedy for the needs of the early Spanish as they ravaged the mines and virgin farmland of the West Indies. As European exploration became more profitable, the African continent was able to provide vast numbers of required bodies to meet the growing needs for inexpensive labor.

For Europeans, the Middle Ages, from the fifth to the fifteenth centuries, was a period in which spices and other goods from the Far East served as the basis of their trade economies. From 1300 to 1700, the Renaissance was a time of religious reformation and scientific revolution. It was a period of cultural awareness, great artistry and the emergence of academic universities. It also was a period of religious turmoil, where Christian and Muslim faiths clashed and wars were fought; religious and populist sects began to emerge, challenging the beliefs of the original faiths.

As periodic diseases crossed the European continent, it facilitated changes in living conditions, diet and personal hygiene. Printed works began to take humanity from the narrow confines of the villages where they lived to discussions on a much broader scale. Almanacs were printed, predicting weather, providing medical tips and showcasing maps that aligned with the stars.

As mapmaking improved, traders began to record and document information about their travels, including key coordinates in northern Africa and Asia. Instruments were invented that allowed merchants and traders to find their way more consistently than ever before. Mighty ships were built that could hold large numbers of men and sail greater distances by using navigation instruments such as the compass. By the 1400s, ship designers from Spain and Portugal had begun to design their ships to sail with or against the wind, at greater speeds and with more accuracy. The redesigned ships accommodated larger crews of men and held more cargo, helping to promote international trade.

With all these changes in religion, travel, trade and global perspectives, the advancement of living conditions, technology and commerce became geopolitical conflict. Europeans didn't see themselves as a single, unified Europe, nor did they define themselves by the demarcated larger nation states, as they do today. The European continent consisted of many small nation states, and its inhabitants often had little identity with their neighbors, in dialect, religion or nationalism. As monarchies rose to power and allowed their rulers absolute control over the state and its people, it was from these monarchies that nations and their people became identified.

European monarchies were sanctioned by the Catholic Church, which had a vested interest in the expansion of Catholicism worldwide. The ability to trade with the Far East was controlled by the various European monarchies and landed aristocracy, both often supported by the Catholic Church. Trade between Europe and Asia was controlled by a narrow passage of water separating the two continents and connecting the Black Sea and the Sea of Marmara.

On May 29, 1453, the Strait of Constantinople (now known as the Bosporus Strait in present-day Turkey) was taken over by the Islamic Ottoman Empire, serving a major blow to European trade and the expansion of Catholicism. Prohibited from trade, European nations sought other routes to the Asian spice and rare commodity markets of Persia, China and India.

As Islamic armies were strengthening their strategic hold on the Strait of Constantinople, Pope Nicholas V wrote a papal bull (the church's term for an official proclamation) to King Alfonso V of Portugal, authorizing him to attack the Ottomans and prevent the expansion of Islam in North Africa. The bull, known as the *Dum Diversas*, authorized a Portuguese expedition against the Saracens (Muslims)[49] of North Africa and granted a plenary indulgence to all who went on the campaign. The pope's papal bull granted King Alfonso V the right to confiscate all the lands and property of any Saracen rulers he might subjugate, as well as authorizing him to reduce such conquered persons to "perpetual servitude."[50]

Bishop Nicholas

Servant of the Servants of God. For the perpetual memory of this act:

To the dearest son in Christ Alfonse, illustrious King of Portugal and the Algarbians, Greetings and Apostolic Blessing

...As we indeed understand from your pious and Christian desire, you intend to subjugate the enemies of Christ, namely the Saracens, and bring [them] back, with powerful arm, to the faith of Christ, if the authority of Apostolic See supported you in this. Therefore we consider, that those rising against the Catholic faith and struggling to extinguish Christian Religion must be resisted by the faithful of Christ with courage and firmness, so that the faithful themselves, inflamed by the ardor of faith and armed with courage to be able to hate their intention, not only to go against the intention, if they prevent unjust attempts of force, but with the help of God whose soldiers they are, they stop the endeavors of the faithless, we, fortified with divine love, summoned by the charity of Christians and bound by the duty of our pastoral office, which concerns the integrity and spread of faith for which Christ our God shed his blood, wishing to encourage the vigor of the faithful and Your Royal Majesty in the most sacred intention of this kind, we grant to you full and free power, through the Apostolic authority by this edict, to invade, conquer, fight, subjugate the Saracens and pagans, and other infidels and other enemies of Christ, and wherever established their Kingdoms, Duchies, Royal Palaces, Principalities and other dominions, lands, places, estates, camps and any other possessions, mobile and immo2bile goods found in all these places and held in whatever name, and held and possessed by the same Saracens, Pagans, infidels, and the enemies of Christ, also realms, duchies, royal palaces, principalities and other dominions, lands, places, estates, camps, possessions of the king or prince or of the kings or princes, and to lead their persons in perpetual servitude, and to apply and appropriate realms, duchies, royal palaces, principalities and other dominions, possessions and goods of this kind to you and your use and your successors the Kings of Portugal...

It was through the *Dum Diversas* that the colonization of Africa and the enslavement of millions and millions of people were sanctioned and sanctified. Through the years, historians and theologians have questioned and debated the role of the Catholic Church in Western colonization and slavery. A recent 2011 English interpretation of the Latin text of the *Dum Diversas* provides insight as to how and why the Portuguese believed they had "ownership" rights to the western coast of Africa and to its people.

WHILE RELIGIOUS AND NONSECTARIAN scholars have and will continue to debate the purpose and intent of the phrase "perpetual servitude," its residual effects were clear in world history, especially in Western civilization. On January 8, 1455, Pope Nicholas V wrote a second papal bull; its objective was to forbid other Christian nations from infringing on the king of Portugal's rights of trade and colonization in these regions. The *Romanus Pontifex* to Portugal's King Alfonso V confirmed Portugal's authority over the lands south of Africa's Cape Bojador and King Alfono's right to enslave its people:

Since we had formerly by other letters of ours granted among other things free and ample faculty to the aforesaid King Alfonso—to invade, search out, capture, vanquish, and subdue all Saracens and pagans whatsoever, and other enemies of Christ wheresoever placed, and the kingdoms, dukedoms, principalities, dominions, possessions, and all movable and immovable goods whatsoever held and possessed by them and to reduce their persons to perpetual slavery, and to apply and appropriate to himself and his successors the kingdoms, dukedoms, counties, principalities, dominions, possessions, and goods, and to convert them to his and their use and profit—by having secured the said faculty, the said King Alfonso, or, by his authority, the aforesaid infante, justly and lawfully has acquired and possessed, and doth possess, these islands, lands, harbors, and seas, and they do of right belong and pertain to the said King Alfonso and his successors, nor without special license from King Alfonso and his successors themselves has any other even of the faithful of Christ been entitled hitherto, nor is he by any means now entitled lawfully to meddle therewith.

Romanus Pontifex *of Pope Nicolas*[51]

In 1492, Spanish monarchs King Ferdinand II of Argon, along with his second cousin and wife, Queen Isabella I of Castile, successfully brought under their control the Muslim kingdom of Granada and restored the Iberian Peninsula as a unified Catholic state. The conflict had been going on for a decade, with Spain being supported by Pope Sixtus IV. In 1492, Granada surrendered. An ecstatic King Ferdinand wrote to the pope:

Your Holiness has such good fourtune, after many travails, expenditures and deaths, and outpouring of the blood of our subjects and citizens, this kingdom of Granada which for 780 years was occupied by the infidels, that in your day and with your aid the victory has been won…to the glory of God and the exaltation of our holy Catholic faith.[52]

With the Ottoman triumph at Constantinople, the Spanish crown feared that the Turks might move through North Africa and penetrate Europe from the west or from the south. Ferdinand and Isabella played upon that sentiment. The king and queen then took further steps to expel all the Moors and Jews from Spain. The Spanish started to make inroads into North Africa, in part to gain economic benefits but also to progress eastward in the stated hope of reaching the Far East, as well as to secure their southern border from invasion. It was during 1492, within months of the conquest of Granada, that King Ferdinand and Queen Isabella signed and sealed documents to authorize the commission of Christopher Columbus to find a western route to the Far East.[53]

After Columbus sailed for the Spanish crown and "discovered" America, the Portuguese and Spanish crowns quarreled over the right to colonize these new lands in the Atlantic Ocean. In 1493, Pope Alexander VI issued an edict to resolve the conflict by drawing on a map a line that divided the Atlantic Ocean down the middle.

The Spaniards were given the rights to newly discovered lands to the west, and the Portuguese were given the newly discovered lands to the east of the line, which now included all of Africa. The Treaty of Tordesillas was signed on June 7, 1494, with both countries agreeing that they could not claim any lands previously claimed by another Christian ruler. This, in part, was the beginning of sub-Saharan Africans becoming indoctrinated in the Portuguese culture, language and religion, as evidenced by the Angolans from the *San Juan Bautista* who arrived in America in 1619.

The treaty now advanced the interests of Spain to colonize the lands discovered by Christopher Columbus, primarily in what was referred to as the West Indies, islands found in the Caribbean Sea, the southernmost peninsula of North America (what is now Florida) and the massive land mass of South America (outside of what is now Brazil). Portugal advanced its interests in that portion of South America allocated to it (what is now Brazil) and most of West Africa. The two nations, with the map drawn by the Treaty of Tordesillas, also colonized the lands in Asia and India.

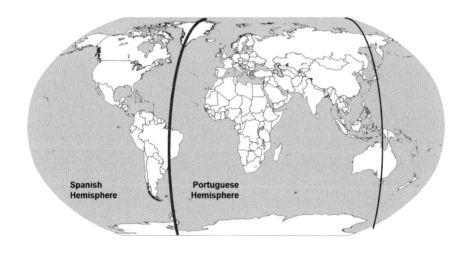

Table 1: Portuguese versus Spanish Colonization[1]

Continent	Portugal	Spain		
Africa	• Angola • Cape Verde • Guinea-Bissau • Mozambique • Principe Ceuta • Sao Tome	• Western Sahara • Equatorial Guinea • Morocco (parts of)		
Asia	• India and Pakistan coastal settlements • Indonesia island of Timor • Macau (Southern China) • Thailand (parts of) • Indonesia (parts of) • Sri Lanka • the Maldives	• Carolines Islands • Guam • Marianas Islands • Philippines		
South America	• Brazil • Suriname (parts of) • Uruguay (parts of)	• Argentina • Bolivia • Chile • Colombia • Dominican Republic • Ecuador	• El Salvador • Guatemala • Haiti • Honduras • Mexico • Nicaragua • Panama Costa	• Paraguay • Peru • Puerto Rico • Rica Cuba • United States (parts of) • Uruguay • Venezuela

---

[1] Portuguese and Spanish colonization during the colonial period may not necessarily reflect present-day boundaries and land borders. The Portuguese and the Spanish empires included at varying times territories on the Asian, African, North and South American continents.

In 1483, nine years before Christopher Columbus arrived in what he believed to be the western half of India, or the West Indies, the Portuguese began to explore the interior of Africa, looking for a possible water route to India to enhance trade routes. Upon traveling the rivers and tributaries of western Africa, the explorers brought Christian missionaries with them who wanted to convert the continent's inhabitants.

One of the first voyagers was Portuguese explorer Diogo Cão, who, while sailing into the Kongo River, first met the Bantu people. The Bantus (*Bantu* means "many people") spoke variations of the Kimbundu language. They were "an advanced, permanently settled farming and herding people who forged iron tools and weapons, and who lived in the same towns year-round." The Bantus lived in some of the most influential and powerful African kingdoms in equatorial West Africa, specifically the kingdoms of Kongo, Ndongo, Loango and Matamba (present-day Angola and Democratic Republic of the Congo). According to African historian John Thornton, the kingdoms possessed "jurisdiction, income raising, military, and legislative functions that claimed comprehensive loyalty and service within its boundaries."[54]

The Kingdom of Kongo had been considered "one of the greatest kingdoms of Central Africa...It covered more than 115,000 square miles, and took much of today's Angola, coastal Zaire, Gabon" to the Congo River, with four million people.[55] When the Portuguese arrived in the Kongo, the territory was located south of the Congo River. According to traditional accounts, the kingdom was founded much like the royal kingdoms of Europe, through the consolidation of power via military conquests over weaker rulers.

Founded by Lukeni lua Nimi around 1390, Kongo originated as a loose federation of small polities. The kingdom expanded through conquered territories and intermarriage, evolving into a royal patrimony. The capital city of the kingdom was Mbanza, a well-built city fortified with stone walls, which the Portuguese later renamed San Salvador. The capital and its surrounding area were considered a special district and were densely settled.

Centrally located within the country, the capital city was designed to be the major commercial hub of the kingdom from the interior of the country and from the coastal waters. Its location meant the capital could quickly provide aid and troops to all points in the kingdom, which "allowed the king to keep close at hand the manpower and supplies necessary to wield impressive power and centralize the state." The two most powerful provinces of the original federation were "Soyo and Mbata, and included the provinces Nsundi, Mpangu, Mbamba, and Mpemba."[56]

As ruler of the Kongo, the king did not have absolute power, but he exercised tremendous authority. He ruled over a tributary system of authority where trade and power were dispensed based on mutually beneficial relationships and interregional trade. The king would nominate the governors, "who collected taxes and tributes which they handed over to the king. The tribute comprised *nzimbu* (shells used as money), raffia squares (also used as money), sorghum, palm wine, fruit, cattle, ivory and animal skins (leopard and lion)." Tributes, taxes and homage were paid to the king in currency, in goods that could be traded and in symbolic items such as leopard and lion skins.[57]

During the fifteenth century, Kongo had a highly developed form of government:

> *The king was assisted by a central administrative body, also subject to dismissal. It included, in the capital, the chief of the palace who acted as viceroy, a supreme judge, a receiver of taxes together with his treasurers, a chief of police, a messenger service, and another officer with the title* punzo, *whose function is unknown. Outside this administrative corps*

there was the lord kabunga, *who acted as high priest, and whose ancestor had been lord of the land in the capital before Nimi Lukeni. Provincial governors were often immediate relatives of the king. The king made his favorite sons governors.... Thus they had a strong base from which to contest the succession when the king died. The governors nominated the lesser lords, who in turn ruled over the* nkuluntu, *the hereditary village chiefs.*[58]

The tribal villages were small and reflected a stratified society that was divided into three social tiers: the aristocracy, free men and the enslaved, "and the aristocracy formed a caste which did not intermarry with plebeians." Similar to the social stratification of period European kingdoms, Kongo "marriages served as instruments of alliance between families, and preferential marriages seem to have occurred. Among the aristocracy former lords of the land, who played the same role in the provinces as in the capital, probably formed an aristocracy connected with other lords by preferential marriages." These connected marriages aided in the unification of the kingdom and helped to preserve and protect the dynasty.[59]

When Portuguese explorer Diogo Cão reached the Congo River in 1483, he placed at the river's estuary "a stone or wooden column, a padrão, which he had specifically brought for the purpose" of marking and claiming the territory for Portugal. After several months of further exploration, in order to ensure that Portugal's archrival Spain or any other country didn't claim the land at a later date, Cão left another marker and then headed home. But in order to prove that he reached Africa and the region along the Congo River, he brought back with him several enslaved Africans as evidence.[60]

In 1485, he returned the captured Africans and sailed farther along the Congo River to ascertain its point of origin. He came upon an area ruled by reigning *Manikonog* Nzinga Nkuwu of the Kongo, "a more substantial ruler than any whom he or his countrymen had hitherto found in Africa." Cão was taken to the capital of the monarch, Mbanza, where he found:

The King lived in a palace in the center of a maze and attended by drummers and trumpeters using ivory instruments. His queen was customarily surrounded by slaves; when she traveled, they clicked their fingers like castanets. The provincial subdivisions of the Kongo were sophisticated, and there was a currency consisting of nzimbu shells found on the island of Luanda, though sometimes raffia-palm cloth was used as well. The

Kongo used both copper and iron, and the women made salt by boiling water. Slaves were well established as one of several kinds of tribute, but the monarchy had not been tempted to trade them on the large scale.[61]

The Portuguese explorers quickly developed a diplomatic relationship with the Kongo king; Cão hoped the relationship would provide them with a profitable trade in gold, copper, silver and spices. He ceremonially recognized the Kongolese monarch as a "brother-in-arms" and an ally. In the spirit of this newfound alliance, King Nzinga, facing several revolts in his kingdom, graciously hosted his guests, hoping that they would help to support his efforts to stay in control of his vast kingdom. In order to show his good faith:

King Nzinga allowed [the Portuguese] *to leave four missionaries behind in his empire and sent four dignitaries with them in exchange. When the latter returned a few years later with weird and wonderful stories about distant Portugal, the king burned with the desire to learn the Europeans' secrets.*[62]

King Nzinga was amazed at the stories and knowledge brought to him by his foreign guests. He was particularly interested in this new religion they spoke of and how it could benefit him as a leader, as well as benefitting his people. On May 3, 1491, King Nzinga was baptized as King João I, along with six chiefs who took names of prominent Portuguese noblemen.[63]

This began a long history of diplomatic and religious exchange programs between the two nations. The Portuguese were successful in converting the Africans

by sending missionaries and [seeking] *to educate some Kongolese young men in the fundamentals of Christianity at the Monastery of São Eloi and elsewhere in Lisbon. By sending craftsmen, agricultural laborers, masons, and even housewives…from Portugal to Kongo to give lessons in carpentry, building, and housekeeping…and by sending two printers from Nuremberg traveled to São Tomé, probably intending to work for the Kongolese.*[64]

As Portugal's relationship with the Kongolese was growing, the relationship between Portugal and Spain was becoming strained. Spain and Portugal, the two great nautical nations at the time, both regularly sent explorers to find new lands to conquer and colonize; thus, the nations often claimed the same newly discovered lands. In 1494, once Pope Alexander VI's Treaty of Tordesillas was signed, dividing the world into equitable sections to be controlled only by Portugal and Spain, Portugal aggressively pursued a policy of exploration and colonization and invested resources to firmly stake its claim on western Africa.

The relationship between the Portuguese and the Kongolese initially benefited both parties. The Portuguese had access to the precious metals, ivory and spices they desired, as well as an ever-increasing number of enslaved people to ship to other growing colonies. The Kongolese rulers benefited from the relationship by being able to educate their people and send the sons of their royal families abroad to learn to read and write and to become baptized in the Catholic faith. The Kongolese also had access to teachers and craftsmen to train their people and to build and strengthen their villages. But most importantly, the African rulers would be supplied with arms and mercenaries to strengthen the Kongolese army against internal insurgents and against some of the more aggressive African nations from the north and the east.

For the Portugese, their interests in the slave trade slowly increased, driven by the newly established sugar plantations on the uninhabited islands of São Tomé and Príncipe off the coast of Kongo. In order to derive the greatest profit from the sugar plantations, they required a constantly restocked large labor force. As plantation profitability increased, the need for additional slave labor from the mainland also increased. Once Portugal and its farmers moved their operations to the islands in the Caribbean and eventually to Brazil, enslaved people became the cash crop from Africa, serving as the basis for tension between the Portuguese and the Kongolese.

Between the late fifteenth and seventeenth centuries, as European states expanded internationally and African states expanded regionally, the monarchies in Europe and Africa became absolute, empowering the rulers with absolute authority over the state and its people. For most of the monarchies, power was often hereditary, causing dissension within the family and conflict with outside forces.

In 1506, King Nzinga Nkuwu, the converted King João I, passed away, igniting a bloody succession when many of his sons and relatives, supported by their various factions, sought the monarchy.

Supported by the Portuguese and their vested interests, Mvemba a Nzinga inherited his father's kingdom. He succeeded to the throne "by violence, executed or banished his rivals, and put his own mother to death for refusing to renounce pagan customs."[65] A devout Christian, he adopted the name King Afonso I and hoped to maintain the strong relationship with Portugal that his father had.

As king, Afonso "shrewdly gathered from the Portuguese a wealth of knowledge about the wider world of religion, commerce, politics, and technology." He acquired the art of international diplomacy where he "frequently communicated through letters with the pope in Rome and the king of Portugal on matters of state, trade, and religion." He astutely ensured that "many promising young Kongolese men [were] educated in the finest universities of southern Europe."[66] Despite his close relationships in Europe, he was defiantly independent and rejected any notion of accepting European colonization.

The period under his rule was considered the "good period," although tremendous conflict and change came under his tenure. It served as a period in which the Christianizing of the Kongolese was undertaken by the Portuguese, and King Afonso converted the kingdom to Christianity:

> *The church stood for power and affluence….The wealthy had themselves baptized and assumed noble Portuguese titles. Some of them even learned to read and write, although a sheet of paper at that time cost as much as a chicken, and a missal cost as much as a slave. Yet churches were built and cult objects burned. Where sorcery was found, Christianity was obliged to triumph. A cathedral arose in the capital Mbanza-Kongo, and governors in the provinces had churches built as well.*
>
> *The population at large viewed the new religion with interest. While the Christian priests hoped to bring them the true faith, the people saw them as their best protection against sorcery. Many had themselves baptized, not because they had abandoned witchcraft, but precisely because they believed in it so fervently! The crucifix became highly popular as the most powerful of all cult objects to ward off evil spirits.*[67]

King Afonso's immersion into Christianity impressed the pope, who contacted the king, calling Afonso "our most beloved son." The pope paid the highest compliment to the king when in 1518, he made Afonso's son Henry, who had been educated in Lisbon with the sons of other African nobles, the first bishop of black Africa.[68] The pope's appointment of the first African bishop was a great sign of respect and sent a powerful message of inclusion to the people of Angola and to the troublesome kingdoms in Europe.

However, during the reign of King Afonso I, the relationship between the Kongo and Portugal had a definite price, and at the center were ivory, gold and slaves. "As early as 1512, the Portuguese Crown made clear that it expected payment for its services, and stated that ships returning to Europe were to be as heavily laden as possible with enslaved people as well as with copper and ivory in order to repay the necessary high expenses incurred" by Portugal to support the needs of the colony.[69]

By the early sixteenth century, in order to meet the growing needs of the sugar plantations in Portugal's colony in Brazil, the demand for African slave labor intensified, establishing the beginning of the transatlantic slave trade. In order to meet their needs, King Afonso put a system in place regulating the trading of enslaved people from the Kongo. The Portuguese slave traders, known as the *pomberios*, often under contract to meet certain quotas, had an appetite for increasing numbers of enslaved people. Afonso's system forced them to begin to negotiate and traffic illegally with the local provincial governors and profiteers.

Slave expeditions could take up to two years in the interior of the Kongo, and the pomberios, predominantly mixed-race Afro-Portuguese, were sent specifically to circumvent the king's order regulating the slave trade. The pomberios sought out provincial governors willing to be bribed and to sell the healthiest men, women and children who could survive a long journey back to slave ships along the Atlantic coast. The black-market profits made from the slave trade caused open rebellion between the king and compromised provincial governors.

In 1543, King Mvemba a Nzinga, known as Afonso I, passed away, without establishing an heir. His death thrust his nation in a deep crisis. Bitter internal fighting took place between his descendants and the leaders of the other ruling families, causing a schism that lasted generations.

King Afonso I's son Pedro I eventually became the successful heir to his father's kingdom in the year of his father's death. "Pedro I had been educated in Portugal, and was described as a wise prince who had inherited all the virtues of his father, and was a great friend of the missionaries" and to the pope.[70] However, Pedro's reign was a short one mired with betrayal, once again thrusting the kingdom into further turmoil.

The year 1545 marked the end of the relatively peaceful intergenerational rule of King Afonso and his father before him, with Pedro I's rule culminating in the succession of power for three generations. This reign was thrown into rebellion when King Afonso's grandson and Pedro's nephew overthrew Pedro as king and sent him into exile. As the royal families and ambitious provincial governors now feuded openly and viciously for power, they threw the once stable monarchy and the West African coastal kingdoms in the region into total anarchy.

King Pedro I was considered to be "a man of noble mind, witty, intelligent, and prudent in council, an upholder of the missionaries." He was also known as "a great warrior who, in the course of a few years, conquered many of the neighboring countries." While these wars "did not enlarge the borders of his kingdom," the one war that could have ended in complete disaster was with his neighbor to the south, Ndongo.

It was through these wars, facilitated by the Kongo's King Pedro and the rapid succession of the warrior kings, that the kingdom of Ndongo became the inadvertent supplier of enslaved people to the Portuguese. In order to secure the needed labor for sugar plantations, particularly those in Brazil, Portugal needed to expand its holdings and influence with the numerous villages along the coasts of Kongo and its vassal provinces; Portugal succeeded in this endeavor by pitting rulers of warring kingdoms against one another.

As one of Kongos's largest provinces, Ndongo, a major supplier of enslaved people to the Portuguese monarchy, took steps to seek independence from the Kongo, with Portugal's help. Portugal obliged, believing that the heavily Christian province would continue to convert its

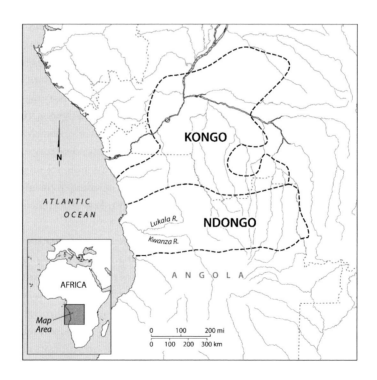

people, which would make them easier to control and thus enable Ndongo to be a preferred supplier of enslaved people.

The first documented Africans brought to English North America came from the West African kingdom of Ndongo, a prosperous region sandwiched between the kingdom of Kongo to its north and the kingdom of Benguela to its south. Ndongo was once a vassal state of the nation of Kongo. The kingdom was inhabited by the Mbundu people and ruled by a dynasty of kings called Ngolas. (The word *ngola* became the name "Angola" when the Portuguese colonized the kingdom a century later.)[71]

Of the loosely affiliated Kongo states, Ndongo was one of the wealthiest and most powerful. It was located on the west coast of the African continent, surrounded by the Atlantic Ocean to its west, the Dande River to its north and the highlands of the Bié Plateau to its east. The Bengo and Kwanza Rivers flowed through the entire width of the kingdom.

THE MBUNDU PEOPLE ALSO shared the Kimbundu language with Kongo to the north. The Ndongo capital city was Kabasa, strategically located on the fertile grounds between the northern banks of the Kwanza and the Lukala Rivers.[72]

The mighty Kwanza (present-day Cuanza) River flowed from the high elevation of the Bié Plateau northward to the Atlantic Ocean, making it a major navigation route for the Ndongos and the early Portuguese traders. When the territory was part of the Kongo, the kingdom became a major trading post and benefited from years of international commerce with African and European merchants; part of this commerce included the sale of slaves.

The royal district of Kabasa was a highly developed area consisting of urbanized settlements that formed thickly populated towns and tribal villages surrounded by a series of complex and sophisticated stockade fences for protection. The royal district was protected and separated from the nomadic and violent Imbangala warriors by the Bié Plateau.

In 1518, the Kingdom of Ndongo sent a delegation to Portugal asking for its own separate missionaries and for recognition as independent from Kongo. The overture was an acknowledgement that the kingdom would agree to Christianize its people as a condition of independence from the Kongo Kingdom. Two years later, the Portuguese sent Catholic missionaries to Ndongo as a first step toward independence, but the initial attempt failed, perhaps due to extreme pressure from the popular King Afonso I of Kongo and from the "rivalries among the Portuguese who lived in Ndongo."[73]

Although the succession of Kongo kings had historically claimed the Ngondo kingdom as part of their possessions, they exerted little control over the kingdom. In order to exert further independence from the Kongo, in 1549, Ndongo's Kiluanji Kia Samba (also known as Ngola Inene) sent an envoy to restore diplomatic relations with Portugal. The second request sought military assistance and offered to have the king baptized, though Portuguese officials at the time doubted the religious sincerity. Although Ndongo may well have seen the overture and the establishment of a Christian mission as a sort of declaration of independence, this attempt also failed.

The 1549 request by Ngola Inene's envoy to restore diplomatic relations with Portugal was intentionally delayed outside the country, by his adversaries. Upon hearing of how determined her delegation was to reach her, once she reviewed the Ngola's official request, Portugal's "Queen Catherine responded favorably by organizing a Jesuit religious mission with a lay leader, Paulo Dias de Novais, who would act as her ambassador."[74] Upon arriving at the mouth of Ndongo's Kwanza River in 1557, the Jesuit Dias and a party of seven

> *sailed up the Kwanza River in a small boat. The barren coastal country gave way to more populace regions with rich valleys and lush vegetation. Numerous palm trees produced wine, oil and fruits, as well as building materials for houses. At the time of navigation, the party was welcomed by one of the Ngola's tribal chiefs. They marched for several days, passing through twenty villages before reaching the royal city. When they arrived they were received by an official…and accommodated in substantial straw huts.* [As reported] *the city was large and well built. The Jesuits considered it not much smaller than their own city of Évora, in Portugal.*[75]

As diplomatic relations between Portugal and Ndongo progressed, Portuguese commercial interests moved from Kongo to Ndongo. Kongo's King Alvaro II now had problems on multiple fronts, particularly if the Portuguese decided to throw favor and colonize Ndongo as their preferred business partner. King Alvaro realized that he would lose one of his most valuable vassal provinces to the Portuguese. He would also lose the key alliance of the Portuguese army, which complemented his own army, as well as revenue from the valuable slave trade. In addition, if the Portuguese were successful in colonizing the powerful Ndongese, it would only be a matter of time before they looked northward to colonize the Kongolese. Alvaro realized that he needed to forge a diplomatic alliance with both Portugal and Ndongo and become a confidant of both.

Although his motives may not have been altruistic, King Alvaro II made known to the ruler of Ndongo, King Njinga Ndambi Kilombo kia Kasenda, that the Portuguese intended to take ultimate control of his kingdom and that the benefits of colonialization may not outweigh the risks, particularly if Njinga lost his kingdom. Once the Portuguese Jesuit envoys arrived in Ndongo, they attempted to convince a now skeptical King Njinga of the reasons he should allow them to set up a mission in his kingdom.

Based on the advanced warning from Kongo's King Alvaro, whether sincere or not, and what he heard from the delegation, King Njinga was not convinced of the sincerity of the Portuguese Jesuit and his seven-member envoy. Ndongo's King Njinga decided to hold the Portuguese delegation hostage. Nine years later, the Portuguese Jesuit Paulo Dias de Novais was released and sent back to Portugal.[76] As a deterrent to any adverse actions by the Portuguese, Inene decided to keep Dias's spiritual adviser, Father Gouveia, who died in Ndongo in 1575.

In a letter written by Father Gouveia in 1565, he provided what he believed was just cause for Portugal to intervene by taking the kingdom of Ndongo as a colony. Gouveia advanced that "the refusal of the king of Ndongo to allow preaching in his lands was ample justification for the Portuguese to declare war and take away his kingdom."

> *He argued that the only way to convert a heathen people to Christianity was by subjecting them to colonial rule. He felt that the Ngola should be punished at once for accepting presents from the Jesuit mission and then refusing to listen to the word of God. His pique growing as he wrote, Gouveia referred to the "insolence" of the Mbundu in their treatment of white men—they had lacked respect for the ambassador of the king of Portugal, whom they had robbed even of his personal clothing; they had accused him of spying and inferred that the Jesuits were a mere cover for his activities.[77]*

While in captivity, Dias had learned that Ndongo had "rich silver deposits in the mountains around the upper Kwanza River."[78] Coupled with Dias's assertion that there were silver mines somewhere in the mountains, Father Gouveia's letter provided the justification for the colonization of the kingdom. The Portuguese made the decision to try to conquer the kingdom of Ndongo. In 1571, frustrated by the strained relations and the diplomatic standoff, the king of Portugal "issued a charter to Paulo Dias de Novais to establish a permanent colony on the Angola coast, around the mouth of the Kwanza River."[79]

In what has been referred to as the "Second Expedition of Dias," on October 23, 1574, Dias left Lisbon for Ndongo as a conquistador with seven vessels and 350 men, most of them cobblers, tailors and tradesmen.[80] It wasn't until 1575 that the Portuguese, with the assistance of their now-allied King Afonso of the Kongo, were able to establish a fort on the island of Luanda off the coast of Ndongo, to be named São Paulo de Loanda, as the capital of Portuguese Angola.

It was from this base of operations that the Portuguese attempted to find the silver mines in Ndongo. On each subsequent expedition, what they brought back to the fort were not silver deposits but enslaved Africans. This served as the beginning of the profitable business of selling Africans as human chattel to international seaports that became the transatlantic slave trade, specifically what is commonly referred to today as the Middle Passage.

From 1578 to 1589, on numerous occasions, "Dias in the Field" attempted to colonize the Ndongo kingdom; each attempt was unsuccessful and met with the strong resistance of the mighty Ndongo army. In 1582, at the "meeting of the waters" between the Lukala and Kwanza Rivers, Dias set out "to capture the reputed silver mines of Kambambe" with an army of "thirty thousand men." But despite the sheer number of men, supplies and equipment, the Portuguese and their Kongolese mercenaries were defeated on the River Mbengu by the Ndongos.[81] Reinforcements were sent, "including three hundred men in 1584, nine hundred in 1586, and another two hundred Flemings, who arrived in 1587, [but] nearly all died soon after they landed."[82]

Determined to succeed and move forward, in preparation for the next battle during the "season of wars" in 1589, the Portuguese forces belonging to Dias and auxiliary forces from the Kongo attempted to install Dias to power. However, at the Battle of Lukala, the Ndongo army proved to be a powerful force, and the Portuguese and Kongolese both suffered heavy losses while fighting the Ndongo, now augmented with additional forces from their recent ally Matamba, its eastern neighbor. During this advancement, Paulo Dias de Novais died in October 1589.

Dias was succeeded by Luiz Serrão, who made another attempt to claim Ndongo on Friday, December 25, 1590. Three days into the battle with the Ndongos, the Portuguese were soundly defeated once again. Serrão was injured in the battle and died a month later.[83]

An uneasy truce was established until another attempt at colonization was made in 1618 by Luís Mendes de Vasconcellos, a Portuguese-appointed colonial governor. It was during this campaign that Ndongo was severely beaten by the Portuguese and their Kongolese mercenaries, and over four thousand Ndongos were captured and enslaved. It was from these four thousand enslaved that the first documented Africans were recorded by the English in the colony's main settlement of Jamestown, Virginia, in August 1619.

3

THE SETTLEMENT OF VIRGINIA

W hen the Africans first arrived in Virginia, many of the colonial leaders were captains of English ships who brought settlers to the colony in different stages. They were worldly, well-traveled men who visited various seaports and dealt with people from around the word who were of different languages, races and religions. Most period seaports were treacherous ports of call, and any successful ship captain had to be experienced in the workings of the underbelly activities of some of the worst of these ports. Experienced captains had to protect their vessels and the lives of their men while negotiating the best terms of purchase for items on board with the local merchants.

Most of the English ship captains who served as the founders of the Virginia colony, "so named by the Virgin-Queen Elizabeth," were veterans of the Anglo-Spanish War (1585–1604), tough men experienced in controlling their ships and their motley crews in the most adverse of conditions.[84] Much like their crew, the founders of the Virginia colony sailed for adventure and riches, risking everything for the profits one would expect for such dangers in life.

As sea captains, often sanctioned by the monarchs of England, they engaged in various forms of privateering, where the primary objective was to steal the property of another for their own personal gain and wealth. These men could be described as cutthroats whose motives and carefully planned actions were often illegal, where the ends always justified the means. They were admired and, in most instances, respected by English nobility because of their ability to navigate treacherous ocean waters and equally treacherous, hostile ports—though often these ports were dangerous because of those same treacherous shipmates. These were the men who founded English North America and would shape a colony and a new nation in their own image.

When the Africans from Angola arrived in 1619, the management of the colony was not much different than the management of a cargo ship; the sea captains merely shifted from commanding ships to commanding a growing colony. Many of the colony's founders left the treacherous waters of the Atlantic only to engage with the treacherous terrain of Virginia. The founders of the Virginia colony, the captains who fought at the height of the Anglo-Spanish war, now came to seek their own personal fame and fortune. Some even used the colony for their own personal illicit activities, including using it as a pirate's den. Although, over the years, historians have portrayed the founders of Virginia as the gentlemen of English society, many of these seafaring founders were far from aristocratic.

These men treated their laborers on land no differently than the laborers on board their ships. They worked them long and hard, as there was nothing else to do on their ships other than work long, laborious hours. They were rough talking, rough acting and knew how to discipline, often handing out harsh punishments for disobedience. Obviously, whatever callous treatment the laborers received from the captains—at sea or on land—was nothing compared to the brutal treatment of the human cargo.

When the Angolans first stepped foot on the soil of Virginia, the sea captains' objective was twofold: acquire as much land as possible and acquire the necessary laborers to work the land at any cost. For the Angolans, Virginia was a new, strange land, a place and society where the ultimate goal was to gain power, land and riches. Though the colony was new, those motivations were not much different than the hierarchy back in Kabasa, Ndongo. However, the attack on the original slave ship, the *San Juan Bautista,* coupled with the legalities surrounding the early establishment of the colony, had forever shaped the role of these Angolans in building this new colonial society.

The arrival and importance of the first documented colonial Africans in the English colony as maritime contraband, rather than as enslaved people, was embedded in the colony's policy for land ownership and headrights. These policies, as envisioned by the Virginia Company in London and shaped by the men who would establish the colony, along with trials and tribulations of the early settlers in the Virginia colony, would jointly aide in the ultimate survival of the English.

At the arrival of the Angolans from the *San Juan Bautista* at Point Comfort in 1619, the colony had suffered from infighting, starvation, disease and Indigenous American assaults. The English noble class was unfamiliar with the intricacies of building a social order from scratch, and the English peasants recruited to the colony lacked the necessary skills of farming and the knowledge of animal husbandry needed to successfully establish the colony. This newfound land was much different than that to which the Europeans were accustomed.

The Africans who were brought to Virginia helped to fill the void of a much-needed labor source but also possessed the knowledge of agricultural practices and animal management needed to make the colony successful. With the arrival of the Angolans from the *San Juan Bautista*, the white settlers of Virginia could not have had better unexpected arrivals in their struggle for daily survival.

The struggles in the English colony were reminiscent of the challenges England faced with its first attempt of colonization in North America. In 1587, England attempted to establish its first colony in America, which included 117 men, women and children who came ashore on Roanoke Island (in present-day North Carolina). The colony was founded during the early years of the global conflict between England and Spain.

During the initial period of conflict between the two great naval powers, England and Spain quarreled over their superiority in the English coastal waters. While England and Spain were engaged in the Anglo-Spanish War, supplies to the English colony of Roanoke were delayed for over three years.

When supplies from England finally arrived, none of the original settlers was found alive. This unsuccessful and expensive first settlement, often referred to as the "Lost Colony," made the English monarchy cautious of trying to establish another permanent settlement in North America. As the battle of naval superiority tested the strength of both nations, tensions between them were heightened by the Protestant Reformation that expanded throughout Europe.

Spain was faced with increasing religious internal disturbances with Protestantism. As a strong defender of Catholicism, Spain's King Philip II was at odds with England's Queen Elizabeth I, the head of the Protestant Church of England, who clandestinely supported the northern provinces of the Dutch Netherlands, which were fighting for independence from Spain. This conflict was motivated not only by Elizabeth's support for the Netherlands but also because she had "given high offense to Spain by rejecting the proposed matrimonial alliance with

Philip, the reigning monarch."[85] Tensions heightened when English corsair ships, sanctioned by the queen, attacked Spanish colonies in the Atlantic and the Spanish ships that imported and exported valuable supplies and resources to and from Spain.

In 1580, as a result of a dispute in royal succession in Portugal, the entire Iberian Peninsula came under the control of Spain's King Philip II. Tensions further escalated that year when England supported Portugal's independence from Spain, after Spain supported Ireland's Catholic rebellion against England's Protestant reform. The Kingdom of Portugal, a friendlier ally to England, received English support in the dispute with Spain over sovereignty. Under the Iberian Union, Portuguese possessions and colonies were consolidated overseas and now came under Spanish control, including possessions in Africa.

By 1585, global tensions had evolved into the full-scale Anglo-Spanish War. Spain seized English ships that were docked in Spanish ports or found in what were declared "Spanish" waters off the coast of Spain's colonies. It was during this period that Protestant England decided to ignore the Treaty of Tordesillas signed by Pope Alexander VI in 1493, which originally denied Protestant nations the ability to colonize new territories. In defiance of the pope's treaty, the Protestant Queen Elizabeth

> granted to Sir Walter Raleigh, his heirs and assigns forever, letters patent "to discover, search, find and view such remote and heathen and barbarous lands, countries and territories, not actually possessed of any Christian Prince, nor inhabited by Christian people, as to him, his heirs, and assigns, to every or any of them shall seem good, and the same to have, hold and occupy and enjoy, to him, his heirs and assigns forever."[86]

After nineteen long, costly years, the war became deadlocked between the two primary monarchs in England and Spain. Upon the death of his mother, Queen Isabella, the newly crowned King Philip III of Spain made an overture for peace to King James I, who was the heir apparent upon the death of England's Queen Elizabeth I. In what became known as the Treaty of London, on August 18, 1604, the war between the two strong naval powers came to an end.

The rebellious Dutch Netherlands, not party to the treaty between England and Spain, continued with its quest for independence from Spain. For many in England and for most in the Netherlands, the general feelings were that King James entered into a treaty with a Catholic Spain without negotiating peace and independence in solidarity with his Protestant neighbor and supporter.

The English corsairs who profited from the Anglo-Spanish War now sought to engage their services with the Dutch, and to fly under the auspices of the Dutch flag. It is under these circumstances that the English ship *White Lion* came to have the Dutch flag and letter of marque, granting it permission to seize the property of the Spanish ship *San Juan Bautista* and its cargo of enslaved Angolans in 1619.

With the Anglo-Spanish War behind him, England's King James I pursued colonizing once again in North America. King James I granted a private investment firm, the Virginia Company, a charter to establish a second settlement in North America, north of Spanish Florida and south of present-day Canada, along the Eastern Seaboard. The charter was modeled after the earlier English trading companies, such as the Moscovy Company (1555) in Russia and the East India Company (1600). The profitable trading companies were joint-stock companies, where shares were sold to private investors.

In recognizing the previous land claims of the Spanish in the New World, the First Charter of the Virginia Company proclaimed that the investors were to make

> *habitation, plantation, and to deduce a colony of sundry of our people into that part of America commonly called Virginia, and other parts and territories in America either appertaining unto us or which are not now actually possessed by any Christian prince or people, situated, lying and being all along the sea coasts between four and thirty degrees of northerly latitude from the equinoctial line and five and forty degrees of the same latitude and in the main land between the same four and thirty and five and forty degrees, and the islands thereunto adjacent or within one hundred miles of the coast thereof.*[87]

The Virginia Company offered the wealthy an opportunity to expand their holdings and their possible span of control in the New World, and provided the middle class the opportunity to increase their wealth, to achieve upward mobility and to possibly own land:

> *The origin of the joint stock company was probably primitive. Its later genesis may readily be seen in the medieval guild. It became an English institution in this application by Sir Walter Raleigh to his magnificent adventures in both honest trade in romantic piracy. The company*

provided an agency for assembling adventure capital and supplying able management to enterprises great moment. It offered an invitation to the industrious to participate in the growing wealth and expanding power of the great English middle class. It supplied an opportunity to small investors, and it limited their liability. It was an adaptation by practical people to practical problems.[88]

The Virginia Company was formed to bring a clear profit to its shareholders and to establish two English colonies in the New World. At its inception, the Virginia Company was divided into two branches: Plymouth and London. In accordance with the king's decree, the Virginia Company of Plymouth was to settle a colony on the land between the 38° and 45° latitude, between present-day Washington, D.C., and Bangor, Maine. The Virginia Company of London was to settle a colony anywhere between the 34° and 41° north latitude, from present-day Cape Fear in North Carolina to present-day New York City. To ensure that the two companies did not compete, they were forbidden from colonizing any land within one hundred miles from each other. Of the two branches of the Virginia Company, the first to succeed was the Virginia Company of London.

The Plymouth Company was initially unsuccessful in establishing a colony after being confronted with a number of logistical challenges. These were the same challenges that confronted Sir Walter Raleigh, who tried unsuccessfully on two separate occasions, in 1585 and 1587, to plant a colony for England at Roanoke Island, present-day North Carolina.[89]

The London branch of the Virginia Company was more successful, and on December 20, 1606, it set sail with three ships from England bearing 144 men, some of nobility, others with criminal records, and adolescent boys, some who were troubled, orphaned or homeless:

*The three vessels…*Susan Constant *(100 tons), captained by Christopher Newport and lead ship in the convoy, was just over 115 feet long. The* Godspeed *(40 tons), under command of the experienced Bartholomew Gosnold, measured less than seventy feet long and fifteen feet across at its widest. The fifty-foot* Discovery *(20 tons), was a pinnace under the direction of Captain John Ratcliffe. Thirty-nine crewmen crowded onto the ships with the hundred or so colonists.*[90]

After a cold four-month winter voyage, on April 26, 1607, Captain Newport, formerly one of the most successful English corsairs, successfully

Colonists landing at Jamestown. *Courtesy U.S. National Park Service; Sidney E. King Collection.*

navigated his three ships into the capes of the Chesapeake Bay. Upon landing at Cape Comfort (present-day Point Comfort located in Hampton, Virginia), Captain Newport, as instructed, opened the sealed box that contained the names of the men who were to serve as the seven-man council. The designated surveyors traveled up and down the Powhatan River (to be renamed the James River by the English) in search of a suitable site to build a fort for defenses. On May 13, 1607, these first settlers selected a peninsula on the James River to build their fort and establish a settlement, naming the location Jamestown in honor of the king.

The James River, its tributaries and the chosen peninsula, once an Indigenous American village, provided the new settlers with the abundances of nature's resources for survival:

> *The peninsula on the James River seemed the perfect place for the colonists to settle. It seemed to be a bountiful garden that provided all of their needs. Along the banks of the James, they saw the "goodliest woods as beech, oak, cedar, cypress, walnuts, sassafras, and vines in great abundance." Besides timber to build their grand city and export home, there was a profusion of "many fruits as strawberries, mulberries, raspberries, and fruits unknown." The variety of game for food and valuable furs included a "great store of deer, both red and fallow. There*

are bears, foxes, otters, beavers, muskrats, and wild beasts unknown."
The romantic vision of the settlers saw fair meadows on which to raise
domesticated cattle as well.[91]

In addition to addressing basic survival needs in this strange new land, these settlers also had the burden of ensuring a profit for the stockholders of the Virginia Company. For some of the settlers, the need for communal self-preservation languished behind the human urge of greed. Infighting and bickering became major problems, coupled with sickness and other health problems, which further weakened the colonists in the face of constant assaults by the Indigenous Americans. These obstacles created tremendous stress for the young colony.

The inhabitants of the colony were all employees of the Virginia Company, and pursuant to the charters issued by King James I, the investors of the company owned the land settled. As specified in the Virginia Company's instruction, the colony was to be governed by a president and seven-member council selected by the king. It was the mission of the council to provide safety, to rule the men and to distribute food and supplies—it was the priority of the Virginia Company that these men also performed their fiduciary responsibilities by ensuring substantial rate of return to the shareholders on the labor hours. These laborers were, in turn, expected to provide valuable commodities to be shipped back to England.

According to Captain Gabriel Archer's firsthand account, on Thursday, May 21, 1607, Captain Christopher Newport "took five gentlemen, four mariners and fourteen sailors to find the head of the river." While in their "shallop" going upriver, on May 23 Smith and his party came upon several men from the local Powhatan federation. They were taken "up the hill to the King" of the Powhatan federation of local Indigenous Americans. According to Archer, they found the time spent with the king and his court to be pleasant and gracious. Archer noted that the king "caused his women to bring vittles, mulberries, strawberries, but the best entertainment was a friendly welcome."[92]

The next morning, Captain Newport and his men met with the King Powhatan and told him that they were going to continue their journey. As the men explored the river, on Tuesday, May 26, they met an even more powerful king, Opechancanough, Chief Powhatan's older brother. As reported, the explorers noted that the king sat in such a "manner… so set his countenance striving to be stately, as to our seeming he became a fool."[93] However, the explorers' initial impressions of this king were

Colonists construct the palisade walls of the original triangular fort at Jamestown, May 1607. *Courtesy U.S. National Park Service; Sidney E. King Collection.*

inaccurate; the Englishmen underestimated his tenacity and strength, but they would soon meet again.

The general pleasantries between the members of the Powhatan federation and Englishmen may have given the English a false sense of security. While the explorers were being entertained by the various tribal kings, in Jamestown, the incomplete English fort was attacked by "400 hundred Indigenous Americans."[94] Fourteen men were hurt, and one of the young boys was killed. The attack served as notice that the Powhatans were a formidable foe.

On June 15, 1607, the settlers had quickly finished the construction of their fort and, according to Smith, were quite pleased that they had "sown most of their corn on two mountains….It sprang a man's height from the ground. This country is a fruitful soil, bearing many goodly and fruitful trees, as Mulberries, cherries, walnuts, cedars, cypress, sassafras and vines in great abundance."[95] On June 22, believing that the settlers were safe and secure behind the walls of the fort, Captain Christopher Newport set sail for England, planning to return with additional settlers and needed supplies. Within weeks of Newport's departure, the men of the colony became sick. By September, almost half of the company had died. Accordingly,

> *Newport's departure from Virginia…and his decision to commandeer many of the colony's provisions for his sailors left settlers, in George Percy's words, "verie bare and scantie of victuals." Except for what they foraged, they lived off a pint of wheat and barley a day. Surrounded by swampland, they unknowingly drank brackish, contaminated water and caught dysentery and typhoid fever. Percy began to chronicle the deaths in early August, some from vividly and aptly named "bloody flux" and others from skirmishes with Indigenous Americans.*[96]

When the English first came to the Americas, there were eight well-defined indigenous American nations. As bountiful as the land was, the settlers had unwittingly selected land in the middle of one of the most powerful federations, under a strong and powerful leader. In short order, this would prove to have a long-term devastating impact on all parties involved.

The Algonquin Nation, consisting of hundreds of distinct tribes, covered an area of modern-day Canada and northeastern portions of the United States from the Atlantic Seaboard to the Mississippi River and down to the northern points of modern-day North Carolina. The people of the Algonquin Nation were nomads who hunted and gathered food in small family-related bands. Much like the invading Englishmen, the Algonquins were a patriarchal society, where property and status passed from father to son. Since they lived on the eastern seacoast, they were the first major nation of indigenous people on the mainland to be directly affected by the widespread encroachment of the Europeans.

Algonquian-speaking tribes on the southeastern Atlantic Seaboard became increasingly less tolerant of the invasion of European explorers and their settlements. As the explorers invaded Indigenous Americans' land, the tribesmen reacted instinctively and tried to overrun the European camps. Customarily, aggression against an Indigenous American village was met with strong resistance. The local tribesmen would either attempt to run the aggressors off or try to capture them and integrate them into their village.

By the middle of the sixteenth century, the indigenous American tribes in what is now the state of Virginia belonged to three language families: the Algonquian, the Iroquoian and the Siouan. The Algonquian tribes occupied the land in Virginia that was east of a line running from present-day Washington, D.C., through Fredericksburg, Richmond and Petersburg,

Virginia, as well as into coastal North Carolina. By the end of the sixteenth century, the powerful Chief Powhatan had conquered most of the Algonquian tribes in modern-day Virginia, creating an empire that included more than thirty provinces under his rule.[97] The Powhatan Confederacy became one of the largest Algonquian tribes and is believed to be the inspiration for the name of the Potomac River. Chief Powhatan's powerful reign continued through the beginning of the seventeenth century.

During the last quarter of the sixteenth century, the Powhatan Confederacy saw numerous European ships from Spain, France and England anchor in the Chesapeake Bay in search of fresh water, firewood and trade. By 1607, Chief Powhatan was reported to be in his sixties.[98] Despite his advanced years, he was a skilled warrior with much experience in battle and in managing his growing empire. When the English arrived with three ships and more than 100 passengers, they had little knowledge of Chief Powhatan or his 14,000 subjects, 3,200 of them warriors. Britain's goal, much like Spain before it, was to extract gold and silver from the land and to develop vast personal fortunes from land acquisitions.[99]

It wasn't long before Chief Powhatan realized that the English planned to take over his land, diminishing his power and control. As the steward of his ancestor's tribal land, he would not allow this to happen. The Powhatan Confederacy was the protector of its villages, their neighbors and their families. It was their duty, at all costs, to stem the invading English tide.

In December 1607, while foraging for food, a group of men led by Captain Smith was captured by Opechancanough and his warriors. Smith and his party were taken to meet Powhatan, chief of the consolidated nations. It was during this encounter that Smith, "through the intercession of [Powhatan's daughter] Pocahontas," was released.[100]

Within the month of Smith's release, on January 7, 1608, the Jamestown settlement was almost destroyed by fire. Over the next months, shareholders with the Virginia Company were dismayed to learn that their investment almost totally went up in flames. This fire, coupled with infighting, classism, constant assaults by the native people and violent sicknesses caused by lack of food, poor nutrition and water quality, had completely disheartened the English investors.

As spring approached, the settlers set out to improve their conditions after a long, miserable winter. They rebuilt what was destroyed by fire, prepared for items to be sent back to England and braced for the upcoming winter season. For the investors back in England, "the prospects of the colony were discouraging. In early 1609, and in the hope of improving the conditions of affairs, the directors in London applied for a more specific charter," intending to recover and grow their financial conditions and prospects.[101]

On May 23, 1609, the Virginia Company received its Second Charter. The new charter would conceivably allow the company to better define its colonial administration and to choose its new governor from among its shareholders. In the hope that the new business model would aid the colony in becoming financially solvent, shares in the company were offered and new investors recruited. Investment boomed as the company launched an intensive recruitment campaign. Over six hundred colonists set sail for Virginia between March 1608 and March 1609:

> *Whatever may have been the specific terms offered earlier investors, those offered in 1609 are clear enough. It was proposed that men subscribe at the rate of £12 10.s per share to a common stock that would be invested and reinvested over the term of the next seven years. Although special good fortune might justify a dividend of some part of the earnings at an earlier date, there would be no final dividend, which at the time meant a division of capital as well as the earnings thereof, until 1616. The dividend promised then would include a grant of land in Virginia as well as return of the capital with profit. How much land depended, like the profit, on the degree of success that had attended the venture meantime.*[102]

Under the First and Second Charters, there was no issuance of land grants to any of the settlers, only vague promises of land. Under this new arrangement, a stratified society in which any adventurer, the official term for those who "invested only his money and remained in England with each unit of his investment set at the £12 10.s per share" but did not travel to the colony, and any planter, someone who did travel to and work in the colony, received the same return on investment, as "the planter's personal [time]... was equated to one unit of investment at the same rate" as the adventurer. Any profits or dividends derived were to be proportionately split between the adventurer and the planter. In order to further entice the investors, either for money or for labor, any land distributed would be given in one-hundred-acre units for each share of stock.[103]

While the proposition of land distribution, at least theoretically, seemed only fair at the beginning of the formation of the colony, in the early years, the colony failed because of the lack of land ownership. As settlers were contract laborers of the Virginia Company, all activities were communal and many of the colonists saw themselves in a tenant-farmer relationship. In the absence of personal ownership of land, along with insufficient supplies, extreme weather conditions and the constant threat of Indigenous American attacks, the settlers were not as engaged in the success of the settlement as they could have been. The settlers were primarily focused on their own personal safety and well-being, not making a profit for a company that many believed was taking advantage of them under extreme conditions.

The first appointed governor under the new charter was Sir Thomas Gates, who set sail from London on June 2, 1609, aboard the flagship, the *Sea Venture*:

> *The flagship was a three-masked ship measuring 100 feet and rated at 250 tons. She would sail armed with twenty-four cannons, in case privateers found the fleet an attractive catch. She could carry some 150 closely packed passengers in her decks and tug a tiny ketch behind her. The vice admiral, the* Diamond, *was nearly as big, while the smaller rear admiral was the* Falcon. *Four smaller vessels*—Blessing, Lion, Swallow, *and* Unity—*were smaller ships that kept in the middle of the fleet. The* Virginia *was a pinnace that could be used for exploration.*[104]

While crossing the Atlantic, on June 24, the fleet was caught in a three-day hurricane. Gates sought refuge at the English Caribbean island of Bermuda. The *Sea Venture* was badly damaged when it came upon rocks along Bermuda's coastline. The survivors of the shipwreck were stranded on the island until the spring of 1610, but the settlers at the Virginia colony were unaware that anyone on board the *Sea Venture* had survived, believing that all were lost at sea.

With the exception of the flagship, the other ships in the flotilla arrived in Virginia with three hundred new settlers and not enough supplies to sustain the new arrivals. Captain John Smith, who was now in charge, oversaw the construction of new buildings at the fort, plowing the fields and harvesting for the winter months. "With all attention centered on the numerous construction projects, insufficient protection was given the meager supply of grain. When discovered, rats had consumed almost all of the vital corn stores."[105]

Despite the fact that Smith tried to bring order and structure, infighting began again, with the stressed settlers constantly pointing fingers at one another. In an unexplained explosion of a highly suspicious origin, Captain Smith was injured badly enough that he was forced to return to England.

Ships that returned to England brought disparaging news about the plight of the colony, which was not what the investors of the Virginia Company wanted to hear.

Upon Smith's departure, Sir George Percy took temporary command of the colony until the Virginia Company sent a permanent leader. Believing that the site for the Jamestown settlement was a poor and swampy location, plagued with disease-carrying mosquitoes, warring factions divided to form new settlements on higher ground.

With their supply of corn and grain destroyed by rodents, and positive relationships with their neighboring Indigenous American tribes deteriorating, the winter of 1609–10 became known as the "starving time," an accurate description:

> *It saw the population shrink from 500 to about sixty as a result of disease, sickness, Indian arrows, and malnutrition. It destroyed morale and reduced the men to scavengers stalking the forest, fields, and woods for anything that could be used as food. The "starving time," appears to have been caused by an accumulation of circumstances not the least of them being internal dissension and the now open hostility of the Indians. The heavy use of force and armed persuasion in dealing with them was bound to have its effect. It cut off badly needed supply of corn and other Indian foods.* [106]

Once Smith left the colony, Percy temporarily assumed the governorship. The journal that Percy had kept since leaving England provides tremendous insight as to the horrific conditions of the colony during that fateful winter. According to Percy:

> *Our men were destroyed with cruel diseases, as Swelling, Flies, Burning fevers, and by Wars* [referring to the Indigenous American assaults], *and some departed suddenly, but for the most part they died of mere famine. There were never Englishmen left in a foreign Country in such misery as we were in this newly discovered Virginia.* [107]

Despite the vast resources and abundant wild game just outside of the fort and beyond the boundaries of the peninsula, the settlers struggled to avoid Powhatan's warriors. Anyone who ventured outside of the fort or the peninsula was captured and killed. Winter was turning to spring, but the winter had been especially harsh for the remaining sixty settlers. The starving time was one of the darkest periods of the fledgling colony. In his

A Dangerous Chore Foraging for Food During the Starving Time. *Courtesy U.S. National Park Service; Sidney E. King Collection.*

book *The Jamestown Experiment,* Tony Williams captures the desperation of the settlers from the letters and thoughts of George Percy:

> *With their hunger growing more acute, the surviving colonists searched the village for food. They slaughtered horses and roasted them....Although the dogs and cats in the village were thin themselves, they were also killed for food, by catching mice and rats the pets were actually competing with the settlers for food. The villagers would have caught fish except there were none to be caught. Sturgeons were absent now from the James River.* [Eventually] *the colonists found a few other items to "satisfy their cruel hunger," they resorted to chocking down the "excrement of man," but they retched it back up....*
> *In such critical circumstances, civilization broke down. They "were driven through insufferable hunger unnaturally to eat those things which nature most abhorred, the flesh of man" but woman as well. Even the bodies in the graveyard were consumed. The graveyard became the cannibals' storehouse. When the dead failed to satisfy their hunger, the living were driven mad by hunger to murder and eat the warm, meager flesh of their victims....One man even murdered his wife and "salted her for his food."* [108]

Desperation and despair overcame the survivors in the Jamestown settlement, and a decision was made to return to England. As the remaining settlers were in the final stages of abandoning the colony, in the warmth of spring, on May 21, 1610, after being shipwrecked in Bermuda for ten months, acting governor Sir Thomas Gates, along with the other survivors of the *Sea Venture*, arrived at Point Comfort. Gates then sailed up to the Jamestown settlement to accept his new command, only to find a devastated colony.

The survivors of the *Sea Venture* constructed two smaller ships from the wreckage during their time in Bermuda; as soon as possible, Gates and his entourage set sail for Jamestown. Upon their arrival, they found a colony decimated by poor planning and the ravages of winter. On the verge of abandoning the Jamestown settlement, the settlers received word that another ship with the newly appointed Virginia governor, Sir Thomas West, Lord De La Warr, and other additional settlers had arrived with enough food rations and supplies for a year.

As the first lord governor and captain general of the Virginia colony, De La Warr arrived to replace Captain John Smith and the original governing council. Upon seeing the despair that the colony was in, De Lar War took dramatic steps to rebuild morale and the physical condition of the fort at Jamestown.

John Rolfe, one of the men aboard the original *Sea Venture* who had arrived with Gates on the salvaged ship in May 1610, had brought tobacco seeds with him. Presumably, while in Bermuda, Rolfe was able to acquire West Indies tobacco seeds from Trinidad, which he transported to the colony. Rolfe immediately began experimenting with the imported tobacco seeds, hoping that the Virginia climate was conducive for growing the plants.

Within two years, tobacco became the first export to turn a sizable profit for the colony. For the first time, the Virginia Company believed that, although the settlers had not found gold or other valuable minerals in significant quantities in the colony, agriculture might actually generate the needed profits on their investments. However, if tobacco was to generate the positive return on investment, it needed vast fields and a much larger labor force to grow.

As a commodity, tobacco was increasing in popularity in Europe, but as a result of the Treaty of Tordesillas, the Spanish crown had a monopoly on its growth and distribution. The English successfully smuggled different varieties of seeds into the colony to test their ability to grow.

In 1611, ships sent by the Virginia Company began to arrive more frequently. In May, Sir Thomas Dale arrived as deputy governor:

> *With him were three ships, three smaller boats, 300 people, domestic animals, and supplies....He thoroughly inspected suitable settlement sites and surveyed conditions generally* [for] *a new settlement above Jamestown which he hoped, would become the real center of the colony. The reasons were well known, Jamestown did not sufficient high land, poor drinking water, and too much marsh. During this period, emphasis was* [to move] *away from Jamestown.*[109]

As the settlers sought healthier places to live away from Jamestown, they planned to build a new settlement on higher ground at Henrico (present-day Richmond) and at Keoughtan (present-day Elizabeth City/Hampton). Once the new settlements were built, the colony began to thrive and spread. However, the expansion efforts only continued to strain relationships with the powerful Powhatan Confederacy. In 1611, as ships brought more settlers and supplies to Virginia, the Virginia Company issued a third charter in an attempt to resolve management challenges in the colony and improve recruitment of investors and laborers. The Third Charter granted the colony a track of land two hundred miles north and two hundred miles south of Jamestown.

The Third Charter provided a short-term resolution to the Virginia Company's problems. The company was granted more land to operate, including the Somer Islands (present-day Bermuda), and was permitted to run a lottery as a fundraising venture. The English rose to the bait; the upper class and nobility who now wished to win favor with the Crown proved their loyalty by investing in the company, and the growing middle class also saw stock purchasing as a way to better itself.

The new charter also provided attractive features to the colonists and current investors. The charter allowed Virginia's assembly to act as the colony's legislature and added three hundred leagues of ocean to the colony's holdings, which would include the Caribbean island of Jamaica as part of Virginia.

Despite its best efforts and the structural changes to the colony's governing documents, the colony was still on precarious financial ground. As more settlers arrived, the fourth city in the colony was established at Bermuda Hundred (present-day Charles City). Although the population of Jamestown rose, high settler mortality kept profits unstable, and new investors were wary of infusing much needed new capital in a business venture that appeared to be a total failure.

On April 13, 1613, while on a trading expedition, Captain Samuel Argall, who would eventually become governor of the colony and a major player in the arrival of the Angolans from the *Bautista*, came upon and captured Pocahontas, one of the daughters of the Powhatan chief. She was brought back to Jamestown and used as leverage between the English and her tribesmen, particularly her father. Around the time of Pocahontas's capture, the first successful commodity to come out of Virginia was tobacco, as propagated by John Rolfe.

Until Rolfe's successful experiment with tobacco, the Virginia Company had yet to find a cash crop that would enable it to recuperate from its growing debts. The tobacco trade was quickly embraced by the Virginia Company:

> *John Rolfe was the first planter on record to domesticate West Indian tobacco and initiate the tobacco trade with England.…Very shortly other planters, sensing the opportunity to profit by its production and sale, began to emulate him. Before long everywhere up and down the valley of the James, the settlers were growing and sending it home to be sold. The ships took away 2,500 pounds in 1616; 18,839 in 1617; 49,668 in 1618; and in 1628, the remarkable total of 552,871 pounds arrived in the mother country* [England] *from its first American colony.*[110]

As Rolfe was experimenting with the West Indian tobacco, he met Pocahontas while she was under house arrest in the Jamestown fort. While under arrest, she began to learn the ways of the English settlers. After becoming interested in the religion of her captors, she was baptized and took the Christian name Rebecca. In April 1614, at the age of seventeen, Pocahontas married John Rolfe, the tobacco farmer. Although the marriage did not end all hostilities between the two races, it did bring a strained but temporary truce between the English and the Powhatan nations.

In late 1615, the inevitable happened. As the settlers had yet to find gold or other precious metals, and with tobacco farming still in its early stages, the Virginia Company was now confronted with mounting debt. Investors were owed dividends on their investment shares, some were owed stock shares and many now wanted the land they were promised for their hard work and years of indentured servitude. As pressures mounted and the company failed to deliver based on expectations, infighting yet again increased between disgruntled investors across political factions. The normal allegiances and divisions deepened, creating financial pressures in England and causing divisions with day-to-day management in the colony.

Tantamount to a modern-day Ponzi scheme, the Virginia Company prioritized settling the profits of early investors. To do this, the company needed more settlers to shore up money to pay out the original investors. Famine, fighting, Indigenous American attacks and a high mortality rate seemed to be the only news from Virginia, which discouraged investors and future settlers. As with any financial model that sustains itself on pyramid financing, by 1616, the Virginia Company suffered further financial misfortune. The original settlers were now owed their dividends in cash, as well as their stock shares and their promised land. Without the necessary cash reserve to honor the dividend payments, the company could offer only what it had plenty of—land. Each investor who purchased a share of stock would receive fifty acres as an incentive.

In an attempt to promote the tobacco trade and the virtues of living in Virginia, in a well-orchestrated marketing ploy, in May 1616, John Rolfe, Rebecca (Pocahontas) and their mixed-race infant son, along with "ten to twelve Powhatans" sailed to England aboard the English ship the *Treasurer*. Within a year of her arrival in England, Rebecca died; she was buried in England.[111] After leaving his infant son with relatives, Rolfe returned to Virginia, and for two years, he "continued to serve as the secretary and recorder of the colony but relinquished these offices when he was admitted to the Council in 1619."[112]

On June 8, 1617, John Rolfe wrote a letter to Sir Edwin Sandys, a member of the House of Commons, and a significant investor, founder and treasurer of the Virginia Company of London, about his departure from England on April 10 and his arrival in early May in Jamestown. As documented in *The Records of the Virginia Company of London*, the letter establishes personal and political relationships between Rolfe, Sir Sandys, Captain Argall and the ship *Treasurer*, each a major player in the arrival of the Angolans in 1619:

> *Upon the 10th of April we departed from Plymouth, and the next day lost sight of the* Lyzard, *having the* Treasurer *in our Company, which kept with us about 3 weeks: at which time we lost her in foggy weather which continued after 20. Days, in which time we had hardly a day to make a certain observation....My wife's death is much lamented; my child much desired, when it is better strength to endure so hard a passage, whose life greatly extinguished the sorrow of her loss, saying all must die, but it's enough that her child lives. I know not how I may be censured for leaving my child behind me, nor what hazard I may incur of your noble love and other of my best friends. At my departure from Gravesend (notwithstanding I was importuned) I had no such intent. But in our short passage to Plymouth, in smooth water, I found no such fear and hazard of his health*

(being not fully recovered of his sickness) and lack of attendance (for they who looked to him had need of nurses themselves, and indeed in all our passage proved no better) that by the advice of Captain Argall, and others who also foresaw the danger and knew the inconvenience hereof persuaded me to do what I did.[113]

As the colony's secretary and recorder, John Rolfe became an important figure in documenting the arrival of the first recorded Africans in English North America, and his prolific and detailed letters to Sir Sandys provide insight as to how and when these Africans arrived. His May 1616 letter to Sandys also substantiates his personal familiarity with the ship *Treasurer* and Captain Samuel Argall, who was part owner of the ship. Upon their return to Virginia, Captain Argall served a two-year term as governor, until he was replaced by Sir George Yeardley in April 1619.

Prior to Yeardley's arrival in Virginia on November 18, 1618, to aid the failing Virginia Company and its struggling colony in America, a set of instructions were provided to the newly appointed governor. Two of the architects of the instructions, known as the "Great Charter," were Thomas Smythe and Edwin Sandys, who sought to

establish a set of policies that would achieve the exclusive profitability consistent with those originally envisioned as part of the entrepreneurial mission of the colony. If this was to be accomplished, real changes would have to be made. The ensuing reforms fundamentally shifted the colony away from a military form of organization to a model of free enterprise. The greatest challenge to the failing company was how to attract settlers and investors to a colony with the disastrous reputation in England because of the deathly conditions, draconian set of laws, and pitiful economic returns. The company decided to offer the traditional guarantees of the common law—liberty and self-government—and greater opportunity for those seeking a new life.

Of greatest significance to drawing migrants to Jamestown with the opportunity of owning private property, the new charter stated that any settlers who helped organize Jamestown before April 1616 would be granted 100 acres of land "for their personal adventure" and another hundred acres for every share they held in the company. And who came at the expense of the company would receive the same parcel of land. Colonists who adventured to Jamestown after that date received 50 acres of land.[114]

In addition to granting settlers 100 acres for each share of company stock and removing governance from corporate oversight to English Common Law, the Great Charter established a land reform strategy to include founding four townships, each to have its own form of local government; to receive 1,500 acres for public support and 100 acres for the support of a minister; and to build a college at Henrico.[115] Perhaps one of the most significant instructions to Governor Yeardley was that he was to establish a legislative assembly, as outlined in the Great Charter. According to Jamestown historian Benjamin Woolley, the Great Charter served "as a founding document [and] provided the legal basis for what became English America."[116]

In addition, under constant and perpetual pressures from its investors to get the company out of the red and to deliver profits, the Virginia Company instituted the headright system, a way to bring more settlers to Virginia. Investors and residents would be able to acquire land by paying for the passage of new settlers. In return, these newcomers would spend a period of time in servitude by improving the conditions and value of the investor's land.

Sir Edwin Sandys, a leading force in the Virginia Company, strongly supported the headright system, for his goal was a permanent colony that would grow England's overseas territory, relieve that nation's overpopulation and expand the market for English goods. Sir Thomas Smith, as the company's treasurer, had a different dream: the Virginia Company's mission was to trade and make a profit.

In 1619, Sandys replaced Smith as treasurer of the Virginia Company. Sandys believed that in order to make the company's shares more desirable, he needed to deemphasize the instant returns on the investment of stock and changed the focus to national pride and expansion. He developed a landownership strategy that would release land for private ownership and at the same time encourage migration to the colony. Another objective of Sir Sandys was to leverage the headright system and to build a more sustainable settlement; he encouraged settlers to establish a family life in the colony. Initially, sensitive to the risk of moral turpitude in the colony, the administrators of the Virginia Company had sent only men to America.

As evidenced by the census records taken in the early years of the colony among the English settlers, Virginia was overwhelmingly populated by men. The majority of those were young, poor and uneducated, and some were previously homeless or had commuted prison sentences. They committed themselves to work for the Virginia Company in America in the hope of improving their own standard of living. Upon their arrival, they worked long, backbreaking hours, which morphed into low morale, a major impediment to the long-term viability and success of the colony. Sandys and many of the investors of the Virginia Company feared the ever-increasing number of young men and men with criminal pasts would have a detrimental impact on their long-term investments.

According to Philip Alexander Bruce in his book *Virginia: Birth of the Old Dominion*, the wide-scale "opposition in Virginia in 1619 to the introduction of criminals" paved the way for rejecting certain "dissolute" persons "from Bridewell in London, whom the king [specifically] had recommended to be transported."[117] Although postulating that while the Virginia Company's intent was to keep out criminals from 1625 to 1650, Bruce reluctantly admits, as politely as possible, that they regularly infiltrated the colony:

> *If a genuine felon did enter the gate of the colony, there were mitigating circumstances surrounding his case, or powerful family influences had been at work in his favor, in the hope that a transfer overseas would lead to his reform; or he was a skillful mechanic, who would be useful to the plantations, whether with his own hands, or by training apprentices.*[118]

Through his research, Bruce provides further insight as to who was being sent to Virginia during the earliest days of the colony. He further notes that not all were in full command to enter into voluntary indenture service contracts as purported by historians. According to Bruce, by the mid- to late 1600s, "it was calculated that not less than ten thousand individuals of different ages were spirited away annually to the colonies through the instrumentality of kidnappers."[119]

> *In the principle towns…there were numerous miscreants of both sexes who earned a revolting subsistence by slyly drawing idle boys and girls from the streets into the nets of their houses, where they altered their appearance, and, perhaps even drugged them into half consciousness, and afterwards took them to the cookshops, where bands of servants were collected for sale to more or less unscrupulous merchants or sea-captains, who were supplying labor to the plantations in Virginia….There were many instances of parents seeking to recover their children either from the cookshops or from the vessels that were going to bear them away forever from the scenes of their early lives.*[120]

At the time of the arrival of the Angolans from the *San Juan Bautista*, conditions within the colony were slightly improving but still dire. In writing about the *Domestic Life in Virginia in the Seventeenth Century*, historian Annie Lash Jester noted:

> *Governor Sir George Yeardley realized that far too few of these substantial workers, inured to the climate and the wilderness, were satisfied to remain in the Colony. He, forthwith, reported the situation to Sir Edwin Sandys, then Treasurer of the Company, who then proposed that one hundred "maids young and uncorrupt" be sent to the Colony to become wives, stipulating that their passage would be paid by the Company if they married the Company's tenants; otherwise, their passage money should be reimbursed to the Company by the planter-husbands whom they had chosen.*[121]

Without English brides, particularly on the western fringes of the frontier, the men began to consort with young Indigenous American women they had met trading with the friendly villages or had captured during various raids as they expanded westward. Many of these relationships resulted in the first generations of mixed-race offspring throughout the Virginia colony. As the men of the colony demonstrated their ability to work and sustain families, the Virginia Company realized that allowing more women into the colony would make it a more desirable place to live—and a more desirable colony meant more marketable shares.

Under Treasurer Sir Edwin Sandys, the Virginia Company changed its pitch. Instead of promising instant returns and vast profits for investors, as desired by the older and original investors, Sandys wanted to attract and recruit new investors to the company. He launched a new campaign exploiting patriotic sentiment and national pride. He assured potential investors that their stock purchases of shares would help build England's superiority in the world and strengthen its economy back home. He targeted the growing middle and merchant class by marketing their investment in America as ensuring their prosperity in England.

Sandys also relied on the shifting religious attitudes in England. Investments made in Virginia would help strengthen England's standing in a predominantly Catholic global expansion and allow it to convert the heathen natives to the Christian values of the Church of England. Investors believed that once the colony was "civilized," more land would become available, and the headright system that Sandys proposed would enable poor and out-of-work Englishmen an opportunity to enter into indentures, sail to America and one day invest and buy land.

By the summer of 1619, a little more than a decade after the founding of the colony, its fate was highly questionable. Different management and governing models were deployed; however, the colony, from a business perspective, was still a financial failure and on the verge of bankruptcy.[122] The marketing of the headright system was just being fully implemented, and its success was still to be determined. Although the discovery of the tobacco crop gave some hope, the colony and its many plantations had yet to realize a profit, and tobacco farming would require even more labor. The labor shortages in the colony caused by the rapid development of the tobacco economy were exacerbated by the low-level skills of those recruited to the colony. The traditional methods of recruiting and populating the colony failed, and the incentive to have one's voyage to the New World paid for, along with the opportunity to receive a grant of land after seven years of servitude, was perhaps the right combination for England's working poor, creating an indentured class in the colony. All of this was a challenge for the investors in London, the plantation owners in Virginia and the colony itself as the Africans on the Portuguese slaver the *San Juan Bautista* arrived in the hot summer of 1619.

4

SAN JUAN BAUTISTA

In 1600, Ndongo was one of the most powerful and progressive nations on the African continent. Its military strength was able to repel the highly capable forces of Portugal, one of the most dominant nations in the world and known for its military might and naval strength. Ndongo was rapidly becoming known for its international trade, growing merchant class, enhanced living standards and reputation for sending young religious and academic scholars to Lisbon, London, Madrid and Rome. Ndongo's emergence in the late fifteenth and early sixteenth centuries was centered on its capital city of Kabasa.

Much of what we know today about Ndongo comes directly from the writings of the early mercenaries and missionaries who visited the area. When the Portuguese first documented information about the capital city, they described its impressive size as similar to the Portuguese city of Evora.[123]

According to firsthand accounts, the royal city was enclosed in a stockade fence with five to six thousand thatched dwellings that housed between twenty and thirty thousand residents. The city was surrounded by other enclosed densely populated towns in proximity in the royal district, with the rural population tightly settled between them. During the period,

Central African cities were more rural than European ones, so there was a great deal of farming going on nearby, and many urban residents raised foods crops and even domestic animals. Yet the rural areas formed a continuous landscape of settlement, so that when a fire broke out in

the town of Angoleme (named for the French Angouleme) in 1564 the destruction of proximate houses spread for miles and was said to have displaced 100,000 people—clearly an exaggeration but suggestive of the size and density of the general region.[124]

After Paulo Dias de Novais returned to Portugal following an unsuccessful attempt to colonize Ndongo, he received a royal grant to build a colony in Portuguese Angola, where he established a settlement in the peninsula region of Kongo at Luanda that would be named "São Paulo" in his honor. "Although defeated, Dias de Novais was not driven from Africa. He retreated to positions near Luanda," where he strategized "a counterattack against Ndongo." After Dias de Novais's death, his successor Luiz Serrão "sought to invade Ndongo's heartland in 1589, [but] he was also severely defeated by Ndongo."[125]

After Portugal's decisive defeat at the Battle of Lukala on December 29, 1589, an uneasy peace was established between the Portuguese and the Ndongo, until another attempt at colonization was made in 1618 by Luís Mendes de Vasconcellos, a Portuguese-appointed colonial governor. According to African historian John Thornton:

Mendes de Vasconcellos had served in Flanders as a soldier and had even written a treatise on the art of war.[126] *He was sure that he could break through the military and diplomatic stalemate that had halted Portuguese advance in Angola since their Decisive defeat at the Battle of Lukala… by the coalition of the Kingdoms of Matamba and Ndongo.*[127] *Indeed he was so confident that, on receiving nomination as governor, he submitted a memorandum to the king announcing his intention to conquer the lands from one coast to the other and to join Angola with the equally new and uncertain Portuguese colony in what became Mozambique, thus opening a new route to India. In exchange, he proposed that he receive a variety of privileges and honors, including the title "Victory of Ethiopia" for his efforts.*[128]

Determined to succeed where his predecessors had failed, Mendes de Vasconcellos's strategy for ultimate success combined his Portuguese army, the military of his allied partner the king of Kongo and the necessary resources of the nomadic Imbangala warriors from the eastern highlands. The period of de Vasconcellos's arrival was strategically advantageous to him, as Ndongo was going through a domestic political crisis due to King Kiluanji's nepotism; "according to traditions collected about forty years later, the ruler of Ndongo, Mbandi Ngola Kiluanji, allowed the brothers of his wife to commit many crimes that outraged the nobility of the country. In early in 1617, [political adversaries of the king] joined together, lured him into an ambush at the lands of a rebel soba, Kavulo ka Kabasa, near the Lukala, and overthrew him."[129]

Mendes de Vasconcellos arrived in November 1617, just as Mbandi Ngola Kiluanji's son and successor, Ngola Mbandi, was being installed. As the new king was attempting to restore diplomatic relations with the "coalition of sobas who had overthrown his father," the Portuguese "governor soon moved the Portuguese *presidio* of Hango eastward along the Lukala River to Ambaca, a point much closer to the court of Ndongo."[130]

As the newly installed Ngola Mbandi was attempting to restore diplomatic relations with the *sobas*, the Portuguese governor was simultaneously establishing a relationship with the Imbangala, a fierce and adversarial nomadic militant band of warriors, probably from the eastern regions of the Bié Plateau. According to Africa historian John Thornton, not only were the Imbangala a mysterious group of people, but also

> *seem to have been a quasi-religious cult dedicated to evil in the central African sense of violent greed and selfishness. They allowed no children in their camp, killing all newborn babies by burying them alive, and reinforcing themselves and replacing their casualties by recruiting adolescent boys from among their captives. These boys were made to wear a distinctive collar until they had learned the art of war and had killed someone, when they were admitted to full membership in the group.* [Some of the bands] *had recruited so many of its people by this method that only the senior officers were said to be members of his original company; the rest had been recruited through capture.*[131] *Their penchant for cannibalism and human sacrifice was apparently rooted in beliefs about witchcraft. The Imbangala activity assumed the role of witches, whose fundamental characteristic was that they killed and ate their victims.*[132]

The first introduction of the Imbangalas to the Portuguese took place during the Battle of the Lukala River, when they sold their captives to the Portuguese slavers. Recruited to fight with the Portuguese, they were a formidable foe for the Ndongo warriors, who feared their unconventional tactics. Their ruthlessness also upset the sensibility of the region's Catholic Jesuits, who relayed their concerns to Portugal.

Mendes de Vasconcellos, considered a professional military commander learned in the rules of combat, "echoed the crown's concerns (and his own instructions) about the use of the Imbangalas by renouncing employment of those who sustain themselves on human flesh and are enemies of all living things and thieves of the lands where they enter."[133] As governor and military commander, Mendes de Vasconcellos understood the importance of the "spoils of war"; conquering a people did not require destroying their possessions or land, which could be seized by the conquerors. When his predecessors used the Imbangala, the mercenaries would torch the fields before they were harvested, destroy the markets and burn buildings. While their ultimate objective was to leave the captive area a barren wasteland, this approach prevented the Portuguese government from collecting the customary tributes from the captured territory.

As soon as Mendes de Vasconcellos arrived in Ndongo in November 1617 as the twelfth governor, in what the Portuguese now called Angola, he found himself at war. Like his predecessors, Mendes de Vasconcellos knew the Ndongo military was a powerful force. As he began his march toward battle, he realized that to succeed he would need the support of the Imbangalas, so "to start his campaign Mendes de Vasconcellos brought three Imbangala bands across the Kwanza to assist him."

During the first year of the military campaign, Mendes de Vasconcellos, with the support of the Imbangalas, was able to defeat completely the forces surrounding the capital city of Kabasa. "The Portuguese-Imbangala forces capitalized on their victory by attacking the now undefended royal palace in Kabasa, taking many captives, who represented the real fruit of war," and most of the captive enslaved came from the narrow corridor of land "about thirty miles broad and some fifty miles deep between the Lukala and Lutete Rivers, the targeted region of both the 1618 and the 1619 campaigns, and the heartland of the area."[134]

> *The army "wintered" in the city but suffered a great deal from sicknesses common to the central African rainy season (September 1618 to March 1619). Falling ill himself, Mendes de Vasconcellos withdrew his forces to Hango and returned to Luanda, entrusting the new army to his nineteen-year old son, Joao. In 1619, Joao returned to the field, defeated and killed the soba Kaita ka Balanga and ninety-four other nobles, attacked Kabasa and drove out Ngola Mbandi, leaving his mother and wives, in the words of contemporary Portuguese chronicler, "in our power, who with many prisoners and slaves were carried away as captives."[135]*

During this initial campaign along the Kwanza and Lukala Rivers, over four thousand Angolans were captured, enslaved and brought to North, South and Central America. This included a group of men, women and children who soon would become the first documented Africans in the Virginia colony, arriving in 1619 aboard the Portuguese slaver *San Juan Bautista*.

Angered by the devastating events in Ndongo (now called Angola), Kongo's Bishop Manuel Bautista Soares wrote to Lisbon in September 1619, informing the Portuguese capital of the appalling way Mendes de Vasconcellos and his Imbangala forces had decimated the royal city of Kabasa, as well as the deplorable manner in which its citizens had been treated.

The bishop asserted that rather than taking control of the city in honor, Mendes de Vasconcellos "embraced the Imbangala, and he [went] to war with them for two years, killing with them and capturing innumerable innocent people, not only against the law of God but also against the expressed regulations of Your Majesty."[136] The bishop went on to say that Mendes de Vasconcellos and his allies' tactics "brought discredit to the Portuguese." The corpses from this campaign had infected the rivers, and "a great multitude of innocent people had been captured without cause."[137]

According to Bishop Manuel Bautista Soares's letter to the Portuguese king, "some 4,000 baptized Christians from the Portuguese baggage train, some free, some enslaved, had been captured illegally by the rampaging Imbangala in the 1619 campaign." However, despite the protestations of Bishop Soares and of the king of Kongo, Mendes de Vasconcellos served out his three-year tenure; under his term as governor, "Angola exported about 50,000 slaves, far more than were exported before or would be again for some decades."[138]

Many people were captured during the 1618–19 campaign; when these captives were designated for sale abroad, slave traders made preparations to go down to the Portuguese coastal capital city of Luanda, where boats awaited their arrival. Regardless of their previous station in life, each captive was enslaved and stripped of clothing, standing naked while chained together, terrified of what was about to come.

As they watched their homes being pillaged and burned, they were each separated from whatever was left of their family units and grouped into small bands for the long journey. For most, this would be the last time they would ever see their family, standing naked, stripped of all dignity and shackled together for the long journey on foot. Whips were used to quiet those who cried out of desperation, and examples were made of those who attempted to escape or rebelled. They were killed on the spot for all to see, dissuading anyone who had similar thoughts.

As each group prepared to make the roughly hundred-mile journey from the highlands down to the coastal waters of the Atlantic, they were fitted with different forms of restraints preventing them from escaping. The old, the sick, the infirmed or anyone the slavers believed would not be able to make the long ocean journey were separated from the group and slain once the group of slaves departed.

The journey to Luanda was long and arduous; many died or were killed along the way. As they traveled the well-worn paths to the city, they could not help but notice all of the ships in the bay ready to take them to their port of call. So many people were captured from the highlands that they overwhelmed the capacity of the city.

Once they reached the city, the slavers were met by third-party agents who directed them to the slave pens. The slavers dropped off their cargo and received their fee, immediately returning to Kabasa for more enslaved people and starting the process over again. While the Ndongos waited in the overcrowded slave dens, the slave ship captains and their crews prepared for the long journey across the Atlantic.

One of the first of the thirty-six slave ships to be commissioned to leave the port of São Paulo de Loanda was the *San Juan Bautista*, with Manuel Mendes de Acuña as its captain.[139] Captain de Acuña was under contract to Antonio Fernandes Delvas to deliver his shipment to Vera Cruz, New Spain:

> *In 1619, the supplying of African slaves for the American market was in the hands of a general contractor (asentista). Such contractors, after competitive bidding and agreeing to pay a block sum to the crown annually, were given authorization to remove a set number of slaves from Africa and to transport these to specified American ports. From 1615 to 1622, Antonio Fernandes Delvas, a Lisbon financier, served as contractor. He was to pay 111,500 ducats a year for the privilege of importing into Spanish America up to 5,000 but never fewer than 3,500 slaves a year, and only through two ports Vera Cruz and Cartagena.*[140]

When the *San Juan Bautista* left the waters of São Paulo de Loanda, Angola, early in 1619, it was heavy with the weight of more than 350 African enslaved. Many of the captured men, women and children would never arrive in Mexico, and some of those who survived would eventually become the forefathers of today's Americans of African descent.

The transportation of these Africans to the Virginia colony is colloquially known as the voyage of the "black *Mayflower*." While no one ship can claim the actual title, three vessels—the original Spanish galleon the *San Juan Bautista* and the two pirate ships, the English *White Lion* and the *Treasurer*—were instrumental in bringing the first widely recorded Africans from Angola to English-speaking America. Based on documentation from the Spanish archives

> *The blacks brought to Virginia in a Dutch ship in 1619 almost certainly came directly, in two stages, from Africa. In the accounts of the income and outgo of the Vera Cruz treasury for the fiscal year, June 18, 1619 to June 21, 1620, is an account detailing receipts from head taxes paid on African blacks arriving at that port. During that year, six slavers arrived at Vera Cruz. All had loaded their human cargo at São Paulo de Loanda, the capital of Portuguese Angola. Out of some 2,000 blacks they had taken aboard in Africa, 1,161 were delivered alive in Vera Cruz. The losses were caused not only by the rigors of the Middle Passage but also by shipwreck and in one case by corsair attack.*[141]

The first known account of the earliest documented Africans to arrive at Point Comfort was from John Pory, the secretary of Virginia to the ambassador of The Hague, Sir Dudley Carleton. As secretary, Pory was required to report on all matters of interest to the Virginia Company, including the settlers' activities in the colony, the arrival of each ship and pertinent facts about its travelers and cargo. Pory may have also recorded some note regarding the arrival of the two retrofitted man-of-war ships in the Virginia colony, as their attack on the Spanish slaver violated the Treaty of London, signed in 1604 after the Anglo-Spanish War between King James I of England and King Phillip III of Spain. The aggressive acts by the two captains would be seen by the English king as treasonous acts of piracy, and the illegal taking of the Africans from the *San Juan Bautista* would ultimately place England in a diplomatic and international quagmire.

5

PIRACY AND HIGH CRIMES

The men, women and children who were kidnapped and enslaved in Angola to be sold in New Spain were illegally pirated in violation of international law and redirected to the two English ships, the *White Lion* and the *Treasurer*. The two ships arrived at Point Comfort in Virginia separately, and each time, they and their cargo were treated differently. The arrival of *White Lion*, though somewhat suspicious, was ultimately accepted, but the *Treasurer*'s arrival was mired in distrust and clouded with questions of possible collusion and charges of illegal piracy on the high seas against the Spanish government.

This particular act of piracy heightened the "controversy between the [various] factions of the [Virginia Company]" in July 1622 and was brought before King James's Privy Council by John Bargrave, who "declared that he had lost 6,600 pounds through the unjust practices and miscarriage of government."[142]

This particular complaint before the Privy Council helped to provide some of the most substantive documentation on the political rivalries and financial interests of England's upper crust and was tied to the historic arrival of the Africans on board the *San Juan Bautista* in 1619:

> *The spirit of conflict was seen in the entire correspondence, and during the few succeeding months bitter complains* [and counter claims] *concerning the mismanagement of affairs in the colony were made by Nathaniel Butler in his* Unmasking of the Colony of Virginia *and by Alderman*

Johns in his Declaration. *That both of these originated in the Warwick faction has been revealed in the Manchester Papers.*

There were other acts which partook of the same spirit as the interference with the correspondence and business of the company. On May 13 the Privy Council ordered that Lord Cavendish, Sir Edwin Sandys, and Nicolas and John Ferrar should be confined to their houses, a punishment inflicted for a contempt of an order of the council table against the use of bitter invectives, and brought about the complaint of the Earl of Warwick.[143]

Although the English Golden Age of Piracy was some thirty years away, the act of robbing a ship or boat from another country, without the express written permission from King James I, was illegal and punishable by the most severe deaths—hanging or, in some instances, decapitation. However, for many investors the cost of maintaining their ships and crews was quite high, and for their ship captains, the financial rewards and profits to be realized from piracy, particularly in the late 1500s and early 1600s, were too enticing to ignore. Lord Robert Rich II, Earl of Warwick, a major investor in the Virginia Company of London and a shipping magnate, was heavily invested in ships that were often retrofitted for piracy in the Spanish Atlantic, and he hoped to make tremendous profits from the illicit activities.

English investors like the Earl of Warwick and their ship captains were paid handsomely by the previous English monarchy under the reign of Queen Elizabeth during the Anglo-Spanish War with Spain. Queen Elizabeth, in order to augment her Royal Army and Navy, had used mercenaries to help protect the waters around her royal provinces. Many of the mercenaries were funded by powerful families, including the family of the Earl of Warwick. When James I became King of England, the Rich family had become one of the wealthiest families, with one of "the largest private fleets in England."[144] Upon the death of his father, Lord Robert Rich II continued with the highly profitable privateering activities and expanded the family's business interests in America on the islands of the Caribbean.[145]

Once the Treaty of London between England and Spain was signed by King James, the political elite and financially connected openly expressed their distaste. The king's decision and the treaty were despised by the shipping investors, who had a vested interest in the decision because the vast number of ships they owned was heavily mortgaged. After the treaty was signed, the shipping investors had expensive ships to maintain, with little to no profit to be realized, so many of the corsairs made the decision to turn to privateering.

After the signing of the Treaty of London, Spain's ambassador to the English Court of Saint James, Diego Sarmiento de Acuña, the Count of Gondomar, developed a cordial diplomatic relationship with King James and members of the court. To ensure that neither side violated the treaty, Diego Sarmiento de Acuña would report instances of potential violations of the treaty, particularly instances of alleged piracy of Spanish ships and possessions by the English corsair ships.

In order to reap the lucrative benefits of sailing on the high seas while staying on the right side of the king and the law, many English ship captains had to circumvent the portion of the Treaty of London that addressed the issue of piracy against Spanish ships and territories. They would deliberately register their boats with other foreign governments to sidestep the purpose and intent of the treaty. Ship captains would fly their foreign flag and obtain a letter of marque granting them the right to attack the ship of an opposing nation.

Even though England had signed a peace treaty with Spain, several other European nations and kingdoms, including the Netherlands and the duchies of Italy, were still at war with the Spanish monarchy. Thus, they could readily provide the necessary marque to willing English ship captains to board the vessels of their enemy and share with the crown of the foreign government their seized prize of stolen goods.

Lord Robert Rich II, Earl of Warwick, one of the most prominent and powerful men in England, was also quite Machiavellian as a master manipulator and doer of unscrupulous deeds. Rich, a devout Puritan, was the head of a vast family shipping empire that despised the Spanish and their Catholic king. In order to benefit from the huge financial rewards, particularly at the expense of the Spanish, Rich took every measure possible to obtain foreign marques so that his empire of merchant ships could pillage Spanish ships in the West Indies for loot, including gold and silver ore from the mines of their colonial outposts in South America.

The Earl of Warwick, who had major financial interests in the Virginia Company and the subsequent Somers Isle Company (to be later known as the Bermuda Company), developed a well-syndicated triangular trade route between his corporate and financial empire in London and the colonial outposts of Bermuda and Virginia.[146] To further develop his illicit privateering activities, the Earl of Warwick strategically placed key allies in positions of power to protect and advance his global endeavors.

No great fan of King James I, particularly for signing the Treaty of London, the earl, who was politically astute, understood that his power, prestige and family wealth came from the monarchy. As such, he took the necessary steps to make sure that he had spies near and dear to the king and his Privy Council. As a shipping magnate, the Earl of Warwick understood nautical and military terms and took every possible measure to protect his flank.

When some of the Earl of Warwick's ships left the ports of London, they were camouflaged to look like typical fishing vessels going out to sea. Underneath the camouflage, the Earl of Warwick's ships were retrofitted as men-of-war designed for privateering and, if necessary, for combat at sea.[147]

Any act of piracy and aggression toward any of the Spanish colonies was politically dangerous and had severe consequences, but those with money and connections often found a way around these obstacles. Sir Walter Raleigh, with whom most of the upper crust of England was familiar, was a close associate of the Earl of Warwick. Raleigh was famously celebrated as an explorer and the owner of the first patent in the 1585 colony on Roanoke Island in North America. However, he also was known as a privateer and pirate who preyed on Spanish treasure ships, and he, despite his status, could not avoid severe consequences.

While under expedition to Spanish Guayana (Guiana), Raleigh and his men, in violation of the treaty, were accused of attacking the outposts and of other possible acts of piracy.[148] For his crimes against the Spanish, the Count of Gondomar, Spain's ambassador to England, brought to the attention of King James I the aggression toward a Spanish outpost and the illicit piracy activities out of the English colony in Virginia. The highly respected Raleigh, who was on probation for other crimes against the king, was tried and convicted of piracy against the Spanish. For his crimes and to send a strong message to any others considering such piracy against the Spanish kingdom, Sir Walter Raleigh was beheaded on October 29, 1618.[149]

Under pressure from Spain, with evidence provided by its ambassador, King James took measures to rid acts of aggression and piracy against the Spanish in the West Indies and in America. King James's treatment of Raleigh reverberated throughout the echelons of England's investment, business and political communities, and the beloved Sir Walter Raleigh's fate certainly was not lost on the Earl of Warwick or his associates.

The Earl of Warwick's complex business interests were well known, including his investments in the Virginia Company and the Somers Isle Company that intersected with the arrival of the first Africans to Virginia. Following Raleigh's beheading, Diego Sarmiento de Acuña, Count of Gondomar, alleged that the Earl of Warwick had also committed crimes of piracy against the Spanish crown. Warwick's global interests reflected his beliefs that "spoiling Spanish commerce" was a "legitimate, honorable, and patriotic part of his larger commercial interests." This attitude brought him to the attention of the Spanish monarch and eventually got him into trouble with King James.

The Earl of Warwick was powerful and arrogant. He reasoned that the use of the English colonies "as a base for such activities [was] a reasonable privilege belonging to one who had invested heavily in their establishment."[150] Further, the Earl of Warwick espoused that in order to protect what he believed were his valid business interests, he had placed friends in high government positions in the Virginia and the Bermuda colonies, where he could coordinate his privateering operations.

However, the Earl of Warwick's beliefs and actions ran contrary to the views of England's King James, who, as he had with Sir Walther Raleigh, took decisive steps against any Englishman caught committing acts of piracy. The Earl of Warwick, with the largest private fleet of ships in England, needed to take every precaution necessary to ensure he did not suffer the same fate as his friend and associate Sir Walter Raleigh.

The Earl of Warwick's animosity toward Spain, its king and the Spanish ambassador, Diego Sarmiento de Acuña, was well known, particularly among the other investors within the Virginia Company. Also known within the company were Warwick's privateering activities in the West Indies against Spanish territories and ships.

The Virginia Company was under tremendous pressure from its investors for not realizing the profits most had been promised. The company was suffering under the weight of all the challenges it faced in Virginia, as well as the weight of infighting among its shareholders, which in turn caused a deep schism between many of England's most prominent citizens. One of the most notable disputes was between Sir Edwin Sandys and the Earl of Warwick, and their respective allies and supporters, found in England, Virginia and Bermuda.

This division only deepened within the Virginia Company in 1619, when the Earl of Warwick's ship the *Treasurer* consorted with the *White Lion* and pirated the Spanish ship the *San Juan Bautista*, bringing out in the open what everyone knew behind closed doors: Lord Rich, the Earl of Warwick, was actively and illegally engaging in piracy against the Spanish. The *Treasurer*

was one of several set forth by the young Rich under papers secured with his father from the Duke of Savoy. Savoy had been engaged in a quarrel with

Spain, and in 1616 had sent an agent to England in search of money. The agent received much attention from Rich, and in return for a large money payment he secured a commission to prey upon Spanish commerce. It was in this way that Englishmen were able to secure from foreign princes the papers giving some semblance of legality to their depredations upon their old enemy which their own government denied them.[151]

Based on the successes of the Earl of Warwick and his late father, many knew or at least suspected that the family was profiting handsomely from pirating Spanish ships, but there was little proof and very few were willing to come forward with such evidence. Unfortunately for the Earl of Warwick, all of his covert activities were about to be exposed. In early 1619, Lord Rich's archenemy in the Virginia Company, Sir Edwin Sandys, one of its founders, became treasurer, tantamount to the position of chief executive officer.

In coordination with his predecessor, Sir Thomas Smith, Sandys set out to drastically reorganize the government and management of the Virginia colony. The two men sought to lessen the Earl of Warwick's direct influence over the colony by replacing two of his supporters; John Rolfe would be replaced with John Pory as company secretary in Virginia and Lieutenant Governor Samuel Argall supplanted by Captain George Yeardley. Sandys believed by replacing Rolfe with Pory he was reducing Lord Rich's span of influence and control. However, Pory later confessed that he was actually working on behalf of the Earl of Warwick's interests.

Amid this palace intrigue, each of the aforementioned was forced to write letters that defended themselves and attacked their opponents once it was revealed that the Spanish slaver *San Juan Bautista* was attacked at sea by English corsairs. It is in these letters, other sundry documents and records of subsequent court hearings that we find the substantial information on the first Africans brought to English North America.

In 1617, two years prior to the arrival of the Angolans, Captain Samuel Argall was appointed lieutenant governor of the Virginia colony. Argall was instrumental in the earlier kidnapping of the young Pocahontas, the daughter of the Powhatan chief, who later married John Rolfe. Governor Argall was also a co-owner of the ship *Treasurer* and facilitated the usage of the waterways of the Virginia coastal area to be a sanctuary for his accomplice's privateering activities.

During his corrupt tenure as governor, Argall profited handsomely from the pirating of Spanish ships and turned a blind eye to English ships that sailed up from Point Comfort to Jamestown with stolen treasures.[152] As a coconspirator with the Earl of Warwick, their privateering brought tremendous adverse attention to the Virginia colony and to the Virginia Company in London, all of which could have a tremendous adverse impact on the investors in the company if the king ever decided to revoke its charter. These were the major reasons that members of the Virginia Company, headed by Treasurer Sir Sandys, wanted to investigate Argall for corruption and have him removed as governor.

As rumors swirled around London and concerns from the investors grew, Captain Yeardley was appointed to replace Argall. Before Yeardley left England, he was given a set of formal (and informal) instructions on how to conduct his initial activities once he arrived in the Virginia colony. The instructions, officially known as the "Instructions to George Yeardley," included language that stated:

> *Grant 100 acres of land to each of the old settlers who had been in the country…and fifty acres to each person who should come into Virginia with the intent to settle. He was also instructed to summon a legislative assembly, which, meeting in 1619 was the first assemblage of representatives of the* [English] *people ever held on the American continent.* [153]

Governor Yeardley was also given "'unscripted' instructions for an investigation of the activities" of former Governor Samuel Argall and his business partner Lord Rich, the Earl of Warwick, relative to their potential acts of piracy in the Virginia colony. These unofficial instructions highlighted the concern that Argall's allegiance was not to the Virginia Company but to the earl. [154]

Upon his arrival in Virginia, Yeardley followed the investigative leads to determine if Argall in particular had made tremendous profits at the expense of the colony's settlers and the investors of the Virginia Company. Yeardley, realizing that Argall and the earl had their supporters and defenders in the colony, made note of the condition of ships owned by the Rich family and what they had brought or taken from the colony. He was most interested in the ship the *Treasurer*, as this vessel was jointly owned by none other than Governor Argall and Lord Robert Rich.

From his inquires, it was clear to Yeardley that local officials were well aware of the pirating of Spanish vessels and the stolen goods brought ashore. They were also sensitive to the fact that King James and his Privy Council were familiar with the piracy going on in the Atlantic Ocean with his former corsairs, as well as the pressure he was receiving from the ambassador of

Spain. These officials also knew there was a real possibility that the colony could be attacked by the Spanish navy in retribution for Governor Argall's use of the rivers and tributaries of the Chesapeake Bay as the headquarters of illegal piracy operations.

Sandys's instructions to Yeardley were clear: if any of the allegations were found to be true, Governor Argall was to be arrested. Once the *Treasurer* arrived at Port Comfort or Jamestown, the ship was to be seized and searched, and its manifest was to be inspected and held as proof of its privateering.

Thanks to his spies, who advised him that Edwin Sandys and others within the Virginia Company were intent on arresting the former governor, the Earl of Warwick was able to send a swift boat to advise Argall of his impending arrest and provide the necessary escape. The Earl of Warwick also asked Argall to remove from the colony any valuables that could be used as evidence against the two men.[155] The scheme was successful, as evidenced by a regretful letter written by Governor Yeardley on April 29, 1619, to Edwin Sandys. Yeardley had to give the news that the conspirators were successful; before Yeardley could arrest Argall, the former governor had already been successfully smuggled out of the colony and had taken his riches with him.[156]

Once Governor Yeardley concluded his investigation, he sent his facts and findings to London. Although Yeardley had been unable to arrest Argall, Sir Sandys, after receiving Yeardley's detailed and confidential report, on June 21, 1619, commended Yeardley for the thorough information and

> *for his proceedings in the case and concurring with him in the belief that it was utmost importance to Virginia. He was ordered to seize the ship the Treasurer immediately upon its return for an examination of her course and proceedings, and according to his earlier instructions to give full information at once to the officers of the* [London] *company.*[157]

As directed by Edwin Sandys, Governor Yeardley patiently waited in Jamestown for the return of the *Treasurer*. Simultaneously, thousands of miles away, the *Treasurer*'s Captain Daniel Elfrith, in consort with Captain Colyn Jope of the ship the *White Lion*, was waiting off the coast of New Spain, ready to attack any vulnerable Spanish ship with its prized possessions—hopefully, gold and silver.

It wasn't long before they spotted the *San Juan Bautista* on the western horizon, flying the bright white and red flag on its central main mast, the Cross of Burgundy representing the Spanish house (kingdom) of the Habsburg King Philip II. The *San Juan Bautista*, a Japanese-built ship, was, from a distance, an impressively large galleon.[158] As each ship prepared for battle, the two English captains of the *White Lion* and the *Treasurer* had no idea that the *San Juan Bautista* was actually a slave ship and not carrying the precious metals and treasures they desired.

The *San Juan Bautista* sailed slow and low in the water, indicating a lower deck full to capacity. The faster *White Lion* and *Treasurer* were able to approach the slaver from its left and right flanks. After an hour's long brutal battle, the cannon fire from each ship took its intended toll. The badly damaged *Treasurer*, the smaller of the two corsair ships, was able to cut in front of the equally damaged *San Juan Bautista*, preventing it from escaping.

Once the cannon fire stopped and the selected crewmen accompanied their ship's captain on board the *San Juan Bautista*, each captain presented his letter of marque, validating their right to attack an enemy combatant's ship and confiscate items of value. It was then that Captain Elfrith of the *Treasurer* reportedly learned that his letter of marque from the Italian Duke of Savoy was no longer valid. The two English captains soon learned that the *San Juan Bautista*'s Captain Manuel Mendes de Acuña was cousin to Diego Sarmiento de Acuña, the Count of Gondomar—the powerful Spanish ambassador to the English Court of Saint James. Both Elfrith and Jope instinctively knew that their actions may be considered piracy in violation of international law. To make matters worse, they realized that they were not on board a merchant treasure ship but a slaver, carrying more than two hundred kidnapped African men, women and children from the port of São Paulo de Loanda, Angola.

Presumably, Captain Jope of the *White Lion* and Captain Elfrith of the *Treasurer* were disappointed with their plunder. They had expended tremendous energy, risked their own lives and the lives of their crew and, at least in the case of Captain Elfrith, would have to explain why his ship was badly damaged for no real payout, only a cargo of slaves. It was extremely disheartening. They were too deep into the venture now, however, and each captain would have to take a number of Africans on board in the hope that they could sell them in Virginia and Bermuda. Based on several accounts, sixty of the healthiest Africans were taken from the *San Juan Bautista* and split between the two English corsairs.[159]

Having pirated the *San Juan Bautista* and split its bounty, the two captains made arrangements to rendezvous in Virginia, unaware of the antipiracy investigations now underway in the colony. Captain Elfrith in particular hoped that by going to Virginia, he would be able to get necessary supplies and have the *Treasurer* repaired.

Based on eyewitness accounts, the *White Lion*, sailing with the Dutch flag and marque, landed at Point Comfort first with its cargo of thirty or so Africans stolen from the *San Juan Bautista*. Unaware that Argall, a man friendly to their cause, was no longer governor of the Virginia colony, Captain Jope was eventually met by the newly appointed governor, George Yeardley, and his cape merchant, Abraham Piersey.

Upon interrogation, Jope was asked to present his Dutch letter of marque. Jope, aware of his potentially precarious position, provided a full but tailored account of his activities at sea. He advised Yeardley and Piersey that the *White Lion* and the damaged *Treasurer* became separated at sea and that the *Treasurer*, based on its condition, would arrive in a few days. This news spread throughout the colony, and the allies of the Earl of Warwick and Captain Daniel Elfrith made plans to warn the *Treasurer* captain of Yeardley's plans to arrest him and take control of his ship and its manifest.

Governor Yeardley was sent to the colony with specific instructions to help build the settlement and to make major structural changes that would enable the company's investors to receive a return on their investments. This included ferreting out pirates and eliminating the colony from being a pirate haven, but now it had a ship in its harbor with an approved Dutch marque and a shipload of kidnapped Africans. Presumably, Yeardley and Piersey, both in need of laborers to work their plantations, were now conflicted:

> [They] *undoubtedly knew that the White Lion had stolen the Africans from the same Spanish slaver that the Treasurer had also raided. King James did not recognize the right of English sailors to privateer under alien marques, invalid or not, and he would have considered Jope as much of a pirate as Elfrith. But frontier Virginia was not England, and the neglected settlers of Jamestown, like those of Bermuda, frequently ignored London laws and trafficked with pirates who often brought them better merchandise than the shoddy trash sold to them at extremely high prices by company investors who had a monopoly to trade with the colony. Even such reformers as Yeardley and Piersey overlooked the questionable circumstances of Jope's arrival in* [in the colony], *because they wanted his Africans as laborers to plant tobacco and make them rich.*[160]

Although sensitive to Edwin Sandys's orders, Yeardley and Piersey traded food and other essentials needed by Jope and his crew in exchange for the Africans. As expected, three or four days after the arrival of the *White Lion*, the damaged *Treasurer* arrived in the Chesapeake Bay outside of Point Comfort. Aware that he no longer had a valid letter of marque, Captain Elfrith, presuming that his accomplice and owner of his ship, Samuel Argall, was still the governor of the colony, discreetly sent a pinnace to verify that it was all right to bring his ship into port.

Probably in the hopes of redeeming himself after the escape of his predecessor, Argall, Governor Yeardley wanted to entice the captain to bring his ship into Point Comfort and then have him sail up to Jamestown settlement to be arrested and have his ship seized. However, before sailing up the James River as expected, after consultation with the Earl of Warwick's sympathizers at Point Comfort, Captain Daniel Elfrith was made aware that his friend and cohort Argall was no longer governor and that Elfrith was to be arrested once he arrived in Jamestown. Elfrith and the crew of the *Treasurer* immediately sped off with the enslaved Angolans still on board, avoiding capture by the colony's new governor.[161]

Once again, after failing to capture Governor Argall and now Captain Elfrith and the *Treasurer*, Yeardley knew that he had to inform Sandys of the chain of events. John Pory, the newly appointed secretary to the Virginia Company, needed to be careful as to how he would report the arrival of the *White Lion* and the *Treasurer*, particularly the specific events that led up to the arrival of the first known Africans in Virginia. Governor Yeardley and Secretary Pory both knew that if King James discovered that any of his ships or agents of the Virginia Company were further complicit in privateering and thus violating the treaty with Spain, the charter of the company would be in jeopardy and the shareholders could potentially lose their investments.

The first known letter penned describing the arrival of the Africans from Angola was carefully written weeks after their arrival in English North America, on September 30, 1619. In his letter, Secretary John Pory broke the news to the Virginia Company's Sir Dudley Carleton:

> *Right Honorable, and my singular good Lorde: Having met with so fit a messenger as this man of war of Flushing, I could not but impart with your lordship (to whom I am so everlastingly bound) these poor fruits of our labors here; wherein though your worship will espie many errors and imperfections, and matters of low esteem; yet with all you will be content to observe the very principle and rudiments of our Infant-Commonwealth; which though nowe contemptible, your worship may live to see a flourishing Estate: maugre both Spaniards and Indians. The*

occasion of this ship's coming hither was an accidental consort ship in the West Indies with the Treasurer, *an English man of war also, licensed by a Commission from the Duke of Savoy to take Spaniards as lawful prize. This ship, the* Treasurer, *went out of England in April was twelvemonth, about a month, I think, before any peace was concluded between the king of Spain and that prince. Hither she came to Captain Argall, then governor of this Colony, being parte-owner of her. He more for love of gain, the root of all evil, then for any true love he bore to this Plantation, victualled and manned her anew, and sent her with the same Commission to range the Indies.*[162]

The letter was written to deflect the obvious. It was full of platitudes and focused on the improving conditions of the colony, a primary concern in London, particularly after the colonists suffered from disease, famine and Indigenous American attacks in prior years. Secretary Pory stressed the favorable yield of crops and the need for additional manpower from England to further provide larger tobacco yields, another major concern of the investors back home. Although Pory deflected from the main purpose of his communication, the opening sentence of his letter makes reference to the well-known *White Lion* sailing with the Dutch marque from Prince Maurice from Flushing, Holland.

While Pory's letter does not directly mention the arrival of the Africans, it does provide a firsthand account by alerting the Virginia Company's investors that the *Treasurer* arrived in the colony, but as Pory wrote, "the *Treasurer*, an English man of war also, licensed by a Commission from the Duke of Savoy to take Spaniards as lawful prize" had escaped capture. Aware that there was no way to eventually hide the arrival of the Angolans from Africa, Pory attempted to disguise their arrival by referring to them as "Spanish." It is with Pory's initial letter that the stage was set for the arrival of the first documented Africans in English North America, and subsequent letters discreetly informed the Virginia Company that there was a potential problem on the horizon.

Several weeks after fleeing Virginia, the severely damaged *Treasurer* arrived in the English colony of Bermuda with twenty-nine suffering Africans and a tired crew.[163] Aware that Bermuda's interim governor, Miles Kendall, much like Governor Yeardley, was an ally of Sir Edwin Sandys, Captain Elfrith had planned an elaborate story in the event he was questioned about the Africans he had on board. However, familiar with Elfrith's exploits, the Bermudian governor was already well aware of the captain of the *Treasurer*'s purported acts of piracy and was prepared to seize the *Treasurer* and its contents if it came to port, as requested by Sir Sandys.

Now commanding a severely damaged ship, and having arrived in Bermuda, Elfrith had little opportunity to protest the seizure of the *Treasurer* once he arrived:

> *Short on food and water, and with his crew on the point of mutiny. Elfrith reluctantly surrendered his damaged vessel at Saint George's. Governor Kendall and a company of musketeers forcibly removed the* [Angolan] *captives and locked them in a longhouse....Captain Elfrith managed to conceal the ship's documents and papers that would have proved the Treasurer's involvement in the Bautista piracy, and he told Governor Kendall that he had purchased the Africans from a "Dutch" ship.*[164]

The Earl of Warwick, who was also an investor in the Bermuda Company, was annoyed by his relationship with Bermuda governor Miles Kendall, who he believed was allied with his archenemy Sir Edwin Sandys, and used his influence over other investors in the Bermuda Company to replace Governor Kendall with a permanent and friendlier governor who allied with the earl's interests. In October 1619, the Bermuda Company's newly appointed governor, Nathaniel Butler, arrived in Bermuda. Upon his arrival and taking office, Governor Butler immediately reversed his predecessor's directives, unlocked the longhouse and assigned two dozen or so of the prisoned Angolans from the *Treasurer* who were stolen from the *San Juan Bautista* to work on both his and the Earl of Warwick's plantations in Bermuda. Butler also seized an additional fourteen Africans that Kendall had recently acquired from the pirate Captain Kerby.[165] These Africans were also set to work on the Bermuda Company's general land.

Once assigned by Governor Butler to the three different plantations, the Angolans from the *San Juan Bautista* who were brought to Bermuda from Virginia were destined to be enslaved for perpetuity. However, the predetermined fate of some of the Angolans was about to change, as they now found themselves in the middle of a major international crisis. These Angolans were determined to be a significant risk to Lord Rich, Earl of Warwick, who realized that tremendous pressure would be exerted by the Spanish ambassador due to the events on the *San Juan Bautista*. The enslaved Africans, who were now working backbreaking hours on plantations in Virginia and Bermuda, posed a tremendous threat to one of the most important and powerful men in England, if not all of Europe, as his international business empire now expanded into the Middle East. For some of the Angolans, their fate was about to change forever.

Upon hearing of the attack by the two English man-of-war ships on the *San Juan Bautista*, Diego Sarmiento de Acuña brought it to the attention of King James, noting that the attack violated the 1604 Treaty of London. The ambassador made clear that the government of Spain laid claim to the stolen slaves and threatened to recover them by force. The ambassador, on behalf of his king, making sure that King James understood the seriousness of the matter, then requested that the English convene a formal inquiry into the allegations of piracy of the *San Juan Bautista*.

As diplomatic weight mounted on the king, his attachés began to exert pressure on the Virginia Company and its executive officers. The Privy Council announced its intent to launch a formal investigation into the entire matter. At this point, the Earl of Warwick began to realize the full extent and seriousness of the charges to be brought against him, particularly relative to the kidnapped Angolans. Of paramount concern to the Earl of Warwick were the loose tongues of any of the eyewitnesses to the events that led up to the attack on the *San Juan Bautista*, which could tie him to a conspiracy with the captain of his ship the *Treasurer*, Captain Elfrith, along with others in Virginia and Bermuda who had any role in the chain of events.

The deceit, entanglements and conflicts of interest among some Virginia Company stockholders in London and some settlers in Virginia are recorded in several communications between agents in America and the principles of the company in London. The author of each letter worked hard to carefully communicate his own perception of the happenings in order to protect his vested interests and himself against charges of piracy or treason.

It is within the deceit, entanglements and conflicts of interest, along with other mitigating factors, that the first documented Africans in English North America were described, not as enslaved people destined for bondage in perpetuity but as complex pawns in the birth of a nation. As discovered in the colonial legal documents found on four continents, spanning the next thirty-year period, the complicated circumstances of the *San Juan Bautista* African captives made them unique in many ways, including who they were, who they became and how they lived their remarkable lives.

At the time of the arrival of the Africans from Angola aboard the *San Juan Bautista*, divisive politics and religious beliefs were in play in Jamestown, the capital of the Virginia colony, and back home in England. Virginia's Governor George Yeardley had just overseen the convening of the first meeting of the colony's representative government. Plans were underway in England and Virginia to address living conditions in the colony, including recruiting substantially more women for the following year; the disbursement of land through the headright system had begun; and the 1604 treaty between England and Spain was being aggressively enforced, ensuring physical safety for the isolated colonists from Spanish attack.

Evolving from an isolated swampy English outpost in America to a bustling commercial port, Virginia was beginning to thrive, though some of its success was due to the trafficking of pirated goods. The settlers in Virginia continued to be under pressure from the Virginia Company to produce a return on investments, which facilitated deep division within the colony.

Back in London, the Earl of Warwick, the owner of the *Treasurer*, sided with many of the older and original investors who wanted high-growth returns on their investments. Meanwhile, his enemy Sir Edwin Sandys, now the Virginia Company's powerful treasurer, represented the faction within the Virginia Company that looked more toward the long-term growth of their investments.

Sandys and his faction within the company were deeply concerned that the Earl of Warwick's political and religious beliefs would compromise his judgment. Furthermore, Sandys was concerned that profiteering schemes against the Spanish, as well as the opportunistic greed of the Earl of Warwick and his partner Samuel Argall, the former Virginia governor, could put the company in the crosshairs of the king, who could summarily void the company's exclusive charter. Sandys's supporters in Virginia also had their concerns. Up to that point, the colony had enjoyed a relatively peaceful existence away from invading Spanish ships, but the settlers feared that the English piracy of Spanish ships could unintentionally put the isolated colony in physical danger.

The profiteering activities of the Earl of Warwick, Argall and the *Treasurer*'s Captain Elfrith brought the wrath of the ambassador of Spain and the Spanish monarch. These men also acted against the orders of their king, instead manipulating the leadership of the colony and its investors of the Virginia Company back in England. Such acts could force the colony to lose its charter and the financial backing from the investors of the Virginia Company.[166] Perhaps more importantly to the residents in Virginia, the colony could lose the physical protection of the king's navy. Many believed that when the captains of the *White Lion* and *Treasurer* pirated the Africans on board the *San Juan Bautista* and hid them in the colonies, they had put the colonists at risk for Spain to send an armada of ships up the James and York Rivers in search of their "possessions."

As factions in the Virginia Company were becoming deeply divided in England, divisions also emerged in the Virginia colony. In order to "draw the sting out," a second and better-known letter was to be written to the Virginia Company, providing another firsthand account of the actual arrival of the Angolans from the *San Juan Bautista*. In January 1620, Colonel John Rolfe, widower of Pocahontas and the former secretary to the Virginia Company, wrote a more detailed letter to Sir Edwin Sandys.[167]

In his letter to Sir Edwin Sandys, Rolfe only briefly and casually mentions the arrival of "20 and Odd" Africans in Jamestown, "presumably" from the West Indies (the Caribbean). John Rolfe was purposefully vague with the owners of the Virginia Company because he knew that if the colonists engaged in any form of piracy, their exclusive charter to colonize America would be in jeopardy. Trading in slavery could have jeopardized their charter, and the involved parties could be charged with treason since the participants knowingly acted against the will of the king.

While Rolfe's letter was making its way to Sir Edwin Sandys in England, the Earl of Warwick was taking steps to address any evidence that might implicate him in any of these events; he was particularly focused on silencing those who could provide firsthand testimony. As the Africans on board the *San Juan Bautista* were the most likely ones to connect all participants to the attack on the Spanish slaver, it would be difficult for the Earl of Warwick to have plausible deniability.

It is unclear when, how, where or if the Earl of Warwick and his accomplices communicated about or planned to deceive the king and his Privy Council, but the earl began to execute a complex strategy plan that involved accomplices in England, Virginia and Bermuda.

As pressure mounted in Virginia, as the colonists contemplated the value of hiding the Angolans from the king and his men, they also needed to weigh the practical consequences of angering the Earl of Warwick or any other privateer who attempted to bring much-needed Spanish goods to the colony. Though the colonists feared being detected for harboring black market ships in the coastal waters, the supplies provided were often more reliable and better than the castoffs sent from England. In an attempt to mask what was already well known in parts of London, Rolfe tried to explain the mysterious and highly problematic arrival of Africans in the colony. It is with this letter that the most definitive proof of the arrival of the first documented Africans in English North America is found.

As documented in *The Records of the Virginia Company of London: Documents*,[168] Rolfe inserted an innocuous paragraph in his letter describing the arrival of the first documented Africans in English North America:

> *About the latter end of August, a Dutch man of War of the burden of a 160 tons arrived at Point-Comfort, the Commander name Captain Jope, his Pilot for the West Indies one Mr. Maramaduke an Englishman. They met with the Trier in the West Indies, and yes determined to hold consort ship hitherward, but in their passage lost one the other. He brought not anything but 20 and odd Negroes, with the Governor and Cape Marchant bought for victuals (whereof he was in great need as he pretended) at the best and easiest rate they could. He had a large and ample Commission from his Excellency to range and to take purchase in the West Indies.*[169]

It is commonly believed that Rolfe referred to the *White Lion* as a "Dutch man-of-war" to provide justification for the ship's captain to take Spanish and Portuguese prizes under a Dutch marque. Referring to the ship as "Dutch" intentionally hid the true identity of the English ship, which provided the necessary cover for its captain (and owners) for stealing from the Spanish slaver. This license provided the slightest cover to give the appearance of legitimacy but, more importantly, gave a clear explanation of how the colony came to receive the Angolans from the *San Juan Bautista*. It also provided a vague cover for the arrival of the *Treasurer*.

As the profiteers feared, an investigation was launched by King James, who authorized his Privy Council to conduct a formal investigation into the entire matter. The taking of the Angolans forced the various parties in England, Bermuda and Virginia to break into warring factions based on their personal, political and business interests. In an attempt to eradicate the illegal privateering, at a court hearing in London in May 1620 on the matter regarding Virginia, Sir Edwin Sandys argued that the matter of piracy in the Bermuda and Virginia colonies needed to be addressed and eliminated:

> *As the case stands the Somer* [Bermuda] *Islands is much frequented with men of war and pirates, with whom the inhabitant there are grown in great liking, by reason of the commodities they bring unto them, insomuch that by a letter from one of their ministers directed to Sir Thomas Smith and read in open Court the robbing of the Spaniards (as being limbs of Antichrist) is greatly commended. And the ship called the Treasurer after her robbing to the Spaniards…belonging to Captain Argall, there entertained and diverse*

men of war set out to the same end are there refreshed, one Kerby, also a professional pirate as is reported doth haunt those islands insomuch as if there be not a strict course taken herein will be made another Argiers.[170]

With the investigation moving forward, much to the Earl of Warwick's chagrin, members of the Privy Council were making plans to go to Bermuda to meet and interview crew members, Angolans or anyone else with credible evidence that could provide insight as to the chain events surrounding the *San Juan Bautista*. The Earl of Warwick now realized that as he was the owner of the *Treasurer*, the Angolans could make him a coconspirator in the act of committing piracy against the Spanish and in colluding to hide these crimes against the king of England.

The Angolans could provide a concise chronology of the theater of events, including the battle at sea between the two English ships (and the flags they sailed under), the conversation between Captain Acuña and the two English captains once aboard the *San Juan Bautista*, details of what happened once they arrived at Point Comfort in Virginia and, for those Angolans from the *Treasurer*, how they quickly sailed away rather than docking only to arrive in Bermuda weeks later. The Earl of Warwick and his cohorts now launched a major conspiratorial plot to hide and twist the events and the facts of what happened in the Bay of Campeche.

In an attempt to hide as many of the Angolans as possible from members of the Privy Council who were on their way to Bermuda to meet and interrogate them, the collaborators made arrangements to remove them from sight.[171] The Angolans, kidnapped in the Bay of Campeche, then taken to Virginia only to be quickly swept away to Bermuda, were now ordered back to sea by Governor Butler, headed for a return voyage to Virginia.

When Lord Robert Rich II, Earl of Warwick, made the decision to remove these particular Angolans back to Virginia, he based his actions on risk analysis. He decided which of the group would cause little harm to him, mostly young children and those with limited English or Spanish verbal skills; those would remain in Bermuda, for he had little fear of them. The Angolans he believed could harm him were those that spoke enough English or Spanish that they could corroborate other accounts of what had happened in the Bay of Campeche. These Angolans were the ones to be sent back to Virginia on the *Treasurer*. But there was a third, smaller group of Angolans who had strong communication skills in multiple languages and were quite capable of implicating the earl if they were questioned. These five or so Angolans were to be shipped to his estate in England, where he could keep them out of sight, and, more importantly, under his control and away from the Privy Council.[172]

But the Earl of Warwick and his conspirators were concerned not only with the Angolans being transported back to Virginia but also the crew members who were on the *Treasurer*, who could also implicate Lord Rich and his accomplices.

Risking their lives in fighting the *San Juan Bautista* in the Bay of Campeche, only to be forced to travel on the severely damaged ship to the Chesapeake Bay, to quickly flee to Bermuda rather than receive aid and finally to find themselves in the middle of a complicated plot to deceive the king was more than most of the crew had bargained for. When no gold or silver was found on the *San Juan Bautista*, they were disappointed. No one was willing to pay for the Angolans, and the *Treasurer*'s crewmen were unsure, after all of these months at sea and all the political intrigue, if they would ever get paid.

For a number of the crew members, they wanted no part of this elaborate scheme. The crew did not want to be blamed or made scapegoats for something they had no control over. They wanted their money, and most wanted to go back home to England. The discontent of the *Treasurer*'s shipmates was recorded on October 9, 1620; in a letter to the Earl of Warwick, Bermuda's Governor Nathaniel Butler wrote:

> As many "of the Treasurer*'s people*" as wished it were allowed to go home, but were "dangerous tongued fellows," and had "given out secretly that if they were not paid to their utmost penny of wages, they would go to the Spanish Ambassador and tell all."[173]

As part of the investigation brought forth as a result of the allegations by the Spanish ambassador, the Privy Council called four men reportedly aboard the *Treasurer*. In response to the June 3, 1620 hearing, twenty-four-year-old Richard Stafford of Staplehurst, Kent, England, testified that he had known Captain Daniel Elfrith for five years and that Elfrith

> went as Master of the Treasurer in 1619 to the West Indies where he was in company with a Dutch ship. When the Treasurer brought into the Somer Islands 25 negroes the then Governor, Captain Kendall, suspected that they had been taken at sea from a Spanish ship and caused them to be put into a longhouse at St. George's Town. Some were then sold and other hired out by Captain Butler, now Governor.[174]

Another crew member, twenty-year-old John Weston of Oxford, also testified on June 3 that he had only "known Daniel Elfrith for eighteen months, and that the *Treasurer* arrived in the Somer Islands in September 1619 bringing a small amount of tallow and grain" on board. At the same hearing, Hugh Wentworth, aged twenty-eight of Basingstoke, Hants, a yeoman, came forward and testified that he had also known Captain Elfrith for eighteenth months. When the deponents left Bermuda, the *Treasurer* lay moored at St. George's Town.[175]

The most definitive, yet slightly fabricated, testimony came from twenty-six-year-old Reinold Booth of Reigate, Surry, England, on July 23, 1620:

> *He has known Daniel Elfrith for 10 years. In 1619 the deponent went on the* Treasurer *from Virginia to Bermuda and at the end of June 1619 she was compelled, while in the West Indies, to consort with a Flemish man of war, the* White Lion *of Flushing, commanded by Captain Chope who threatened to shoot at the* Treasurer *unless Elfrith complied with his wishes. Chope had permission to seize Spanish ships and in mid July 1619 he took 25 men from his own and Elfrith's ships and sailed away in a pinnace. After 3 days he brought back a Spanish frigate which he had captured and, out of goodwill towards Elfrith, gave him some tallow and grain from her. Immediately after this the deponent left the* Treasurer *in the* Seaflower *for Bermuda and departed from there for England.*[176]

Now aware that Sandys had issued a warrant for the arrest of Argall and Elfrith in Virginia and intended to seize his ship the *Treasurer*, the Earl of Warwick instinctively knew that his archenemy would not rest until they were all arrested. Back in England, as part of his elaborate scheme, the earl and his allies worked to deconstruct the events involving the *Treasurer*, concocting a story that exaggerated the role of Captain John Colyn Jope of the much larger, 160-ton *White Lion*, going so far as to include a story that Jope was the leader of the piracy scheme and forced Elfrith and his crew to comply. They also emphasized that the *White Lion* was a Dutch ship to deliberately hide its true English identity.

The intent of the fabricated story was to divert attention away from Elfrith to Jope, who took over command of the two ships, though most involved were hoping that the whole matter would be dismissed, particularly since the *White Lion* was successful in unloading the valuable cargo of the Angolans in the Virginia colony. Unlike the *Treasurer*, the ownership of the *White Lion* was not directly connected to the Virginia Company and therefore did not pose the same threat to the colony as the *Treasurer* did to Sir Rich, Earl of Warwick.

The whole farce that the captain of the *White Lion* had intimidated the well-connected captain of the smaller *Treasurer* in the West Indies was absurd at best. However, Elfrith and the Earl of Warwick's diversionary tactics worked. Their allies on the Privy Council limited the scope of their questions and extracted only the testimony they wanted from the deponents.

In their testimony, none of the crew of the *Treasurer* mentioned anything about the captured *Bautista* Angolans or the events through which they came to arrive on the *Treasurer*. While the crewmen provided compelling testimony, for what it was, none was asked about the Angolans taken from the *San Juan Bautista* or their current whereabouts. Elfrith's own testimony was transparently self-serving, but he had powerful friends on the Privy Council to support him. Initially, the court of inquiry accepted Elfrith's versions of the events.

However, subsequent period records found in Bermuda and in England clearly contradict the false narrative concocted by most of the key players with vested interests in deflecting from the truth of the violent events on the high seas in the Bay of Campeche. Fortunately for historians seeking to learn the truth about the first documented Africans in English North America, the complex web of lies in fact provides a clear picture of the number of Angolans taken from the *San Juan Bautista*, how many initially arrived in Virginia, the number of Angolans who arrived in Bermuda and, eventually, how some of them found their way to England only to return to the Virginia colony.

The complications and concerns in Bermuda, caused by a number of parties that feared being accused of piracy and possibly found guilty of treason, determined that the Angolans, once in the Virginia colony, were not treated as enslaved men, women and children. They were the fruits of an illegal act on the high seas in which a treaty between two sovereign nations was broken and, as such, were considered maritime contraband. As discussed later, when the ship "*Garland* arrived [in England] from the Somers Islands," it brought with it a number of letters, each attempting to put the authors' own spin on a very complex narrative: "the governor, Nathaniel Butler, sent [three letters to the Earl of Warwick]; Miles Kendal wrote to the [Earl of Warwick] and to Sir Edwin Sandys; and John Dutton wrote to the Earl of Warwick." The letters arrived at the exact time the Privy Council was beginning the investigation of the chain of events. Although "all of these letters mentioned the *Treasurer* as then being in the Somers Islands…the matter was not reported to the Privy Council, or to the Spanish Agent."[177]

In one of the letters, Butler advised the Earl of Warwick that there was a "scarcity of corn," which was the purpose of the communication, for the settlers in Bermuda lacked food and supplies, and the ships out of London were to be used to bring victuals to the settlers and not to be used for acts of piracy. However, in a postscript, Butler acknowledged the delivery of "fourteen negroes."[178] The arrival of these same Angolans was confirmed by later accounts presented at a court hearing in the Somers Islands (Bermuda) on Wednesday, May 7, 1623, which informed the courts that a group of Angolans from the *San Juan Bautista* landed in Bermuda:

> *Violently…contrary to the course of law and consigned into the possession of their potent adversaries, as has lately appended in the case of Caption Miles Kendall who was spoiled by Captain Butler of 14* [blacks] *granted to him by a Captain of Holland (in reference to the captain of the* White Lion*) having commission from the Prince of Orange under a bare and false pretense yet they belonged to a ship called the* Treasurer *set out from Virginia by Sir Samuel Argall then governor to prey in the West Indies.*[179]

The charade of the *Treasurer*'s Captain Elfrith, the Earl of Warwick and Bermuda's Governor Butler relative to the acts of piracy of the *San Juan Bautista*, coupled with the arrival and placement of the Angolans, have confounded historians regarding the specific number of Angolans that actually arrived in Virginia in the late summer of 1619. What is known from the numerous letters that crossed the Atlantic between England and Bermuda, as found in the Public Records Office in the National Archives in Kew, England, is that fourteen Angolans were sent to Bermuda before the *White Lion* arrived in Virginia by way of Captain Kerby.[180] Twenty-nine arrived in Bermuda on board the *Treasurer*, and as written by Alexander Brown in his 1898 *The Genesis of the United States*, the *Treasurer*, having left only one Angolan in Virginia, "soon sailed from there, taking the remainder [of the ship's] [Angolans] to the Bermudas."[181]

The international incidents surrounding the pirating of the *San Juan Bautista* and the taking of the Angolans put into clearer perspective their arrival and status in the Virginia colony. These events would also later serve as a catalyst for King James I to take control over the responsibilities of governing Virginia in the wake of a 1622 attack by the Powhatans and the Virginia Company of London's collapse. King James would ultimately appoint a royal commission to manage the colony's day-to-day affairs, eventually creating additional tension between the colonists and the English monarchy.

THE FIRST RECORDED AFRICANS

When the English first arrived in 1607 and 1620 in Jamestown and Plymouth Bay, respectively, they were well documented. From the time they left England to the time they disembarked, their names were recorded on ship manifests, and they were found in most of the muster/census records. Conversely, when the Angolans left Africa until the time they arrived in English North America on board the *San Juan Bautista*, they were destined to be nameless individuals, intended as nothing more than chattel property on the massive agricultural farms of New Spain or Brazil.

When the Angolans came to Virginia, they could not be found in a ship's manifest or the first muster taken within the colony. When they were traded for victuals and supplies at Point Comfort, and then distributed throughout the colony, they temporarily disappeared into obscurity. For some, their African birth names have now been lost to history.

However, the Angolans began to reappear in the colony in the most unusual ways: through the ledgers of the headright system, through subsequent census records and from the legal documents left behind by various county courthouses. It is from these colonial records, as well as the records of the Virginia Company in England, that we can begin the long and arduous journey of unmasking and preserving their identities and legacies for generations to come.

These voluminous records of the Africans once held on board the *San Juan Bautista*, then transferred to the *White Lion* and the *Treasurer*, reveal the true history and identities of these remarkable Angolans and not the false narrative imposed on them.

Interpretation of the arrival of the first documented Africans in English America. *Courtesy U.S. National Park Service; Sidney E. King Collection.*

Through the years, historians have provided false narratives depicting the Angolans in early Virginia as unskilled laborers with limited abilities, unable to fend for themselves. However, the original colonial source documents derived from court hearings, judicial rulings, personal statements and estate papers provide a clearer understanding of the full capacity of these early Angolans and their invaluable contributions to the economy of the Virginia colony. Further, their ability to defend themselves in and skilled navigation of the judicial system demonstrates the competence of these Angolans; anything to the contrary is a false narrative.

The first census for the Virginia colony, known as the Muster of 1620, lists 892 Europeans and, among "Others not Christians in the Service of the English," includes 4 Indigenous Americans and 32 Angolans. The muster found in the Ferrar Papers was referred to as the "Sums total of all Persons, Cattle, Corne Armes houses, and boats contained in the general Muster of Virginia."[182] The population was categorized as either Christian (to mean whites) or Non-Christian (to mean non-whites).[183]

This census highlights a discrepancy between the population reported to the census and the letter sent by John Rolfe months earlier to officers of the London Company.

It is in the 1620 census that the first specific mention of the original Angolans brought to English North America occurs and where they are documented in definitive numbers. The census, which receives greater attention later, diverges significantly from the Rolfe Papers in terms of the purported numbers of Angolans in the colony from 1619 to 1620.

Although this census does not provide the names of any of the Angolans, presuming that its veracity is accurate, it does serve as the basis going forward relative to their actual numbers in the colony. This census has led some to question the true number of Angolans brought to the colony from the *San Juan Bautista* compared to the veracity of the number of "20 and Odd" from the John Rolfe letter to Sir Sandys as purported.[184]

Table 1: Virginia Census of 1620[1]

Muster		Total
English and other Christians in Virginia:		
Able men	670	
Women	119	
Boys serviceable	039	
Younger Children	057	
Sub-Total		885
Non-Christians in the Service of the English:		
Indigenous Americans	04	
Africans	32	
African Men	15	
African Women	17	
Sub-Total		36
Total Population		921

---

[1]   Ferrar Papers, V.33: No. 3, Summer, 1995, p. 168.

The March 1620 census is a valuable colonial record that enables us to construct valuable clues as to the men, women and children who were transferred from the *San Juan Bautista* to the *White Lion* and the *Treasurer*. The census was an actual head count of the inhabitants within the colony and gives a clear picture of the number of Angolans in the colony. However, the various musters were an imperfect head count based on the commanders of the area being present, reporting the numbers and submitting the information to the colony's court, as evidenced by an example of the April 8, 1629 order of the court:

> *The General Court ordered that every commander within the several plantations of this colony shall take a general muster of all inhabitants men, women and children, as well as* [blacks] *inhabiting within the same and return a list of their names to the Governor and Council at the next quarter court to be here holden.*[185]

If the Rolfe letter to Sandys, which claimed that twenty or so Angolans disembarked from the *White Lion*, is to be believed, one would question: where did the additional twelve or so Angolans come from? The preponderance of evidence would suggest that the number of the thirty-two Angolans in the colony at the time of the 1620 census is consistent with the subsequent List of 1623 and the Muster of 1624–1625, as well as aligning with the number of sixty Angolans taken from the *San Juan Bautista* in the Bay of Campeche and split between the *White Lion* and the *Treasurer*.[186]

What is known is that when the slaver *San Juan Bautista* left the port of São Paulo de Loanda, Angola, its captain, Manuel Mendes de Acuña, was under contract to Antonio Fernandes Delvas to deliver a shipment of 350 captive Angolans to Vera Cruz, New Spain. According to the financial accounting ledger, Captain Acuña, upon his arrival in Vera Cruz, entered on the credit side the arrival and delivery of only 147 out of the original 350. His losses, resulting from causes on board ship, also included the trade of young boys for supplies and medicine in Bermuda and the pirating of sixty Angolans by the English corsairs the *White Lion* and the *Treasurer*. Delivering a little more than a third of his cargo to Vera Cruz, Captain Acuña suffered severe financial losses that nearly bankrupted him.

To account for the sixty Angolans taken from the *San Juan Bautista* and split between the *White Lion* and the *Treasurer*, we learned that when the *White Lion* arrived at Point Comfort, fourteen Angolans were split between Governor Yeardley and his cape merchant Abraham Piersey. The other fourteen or so were provided to other leaders of the colony and then sent

Table 1: Losses On board
the *San Juan Bautista*

	Total
Departure from São Paulo de Loanda:	350
Losses at Sea:	
Deaths On board from Sickness[1]	-119
Traded "young boys" for medicine in Jamaica	-24
Pirated Losses to the *White Lion*	-30
Pirated Losses to the *Treasurer*	-30
Sub-Total Losses	-203
Total Arrivals in Vera Cruz	147

---

[1] The actual number of losses at sea due to sickness or other factors is not definitively known. What Captain Acuña attested to upon his arrival in Vera Cruz, New Spain is that "more than one hundred on the Bautista had died of sickness." See Also. Hashaw, 69.

to the most remote areas of the colony. Relative to the thirty Angolans on Captain Elfrith's ship the *Treasurer*, one woman was left behind and thirty-nine went to Bermuda.[187]

Some historians have postulated that no Angolans were left behind in Elfrith's share at Point Comfort when it landed. However, that would contradict Census List of 1623 where a woman by the name of Angelo (Angela) is found, then the subsequent Muster of 1624–1625 where she is once again found, and the ship she arrived on is noted as the *Treasurer*. When the *Treasurer* landed at Point Comfort, Captain Elfrith sent an officer to shore to trade his share of Angolans for food and other supplies. When the officer went ashore, he brought one Angolan with him, a woman (named Angela), as evidence as to their cargo onboard ship. Governor Yeardley sent John Rolfe, along with Captain John Ewen and Rolfe's father-in-law, Captain William Pierce, to meet the ship. By time they arrived, the *Treasurer* had already taken off, leaving behind the ship's officer and the Angolan woman. Once taken to Jamestown, Governor "Yeardley questioned the ship's officer under oath [at] which time he confessed that they [the *Treasurer*] had been robbing the Spanish."[188] It is presumed for his efforts in bringing the ship's officer and the Angolan woman up to Jamestown, as the senior member of the party, Captain Pierce was given the Angolan woman who we now know as Angela.

Once Captain Elfrith rightfully presumed that his officer would confess to the *Treasurer*'s piracy, he hastily departed Point Comfort for Bermuda without the officer or the Angolan woman. The small English island of Bermuda (Somers Islands) holds some unique clues as to the veracity of the numbers of Angolans in Virginia as provided in the 1620 census, and the island's colonial records offer new clues as to where the additional Angolans might have come from if the John Rolfe to Sir Sandys is to be believed.

Within six weeks after the arrival of Rolfe's "20 and Odd" Africans at Point Comfort, Virginia, four English ships arrived in Bermuda, along with two major hurricanes that struck the island. According to the Bermuda Colonial Records and other original sources, the ships are found in its *Bermuda List of Occasional Visitors, Emigrant Vessels, Magazine Ships, and Private Traders, Arriving at the Somers Islands Down to 1684.*[189] The ships *Treasurer*, *Warwick* and *Garland* arrived within weeks of one another.

During the fall of 1619, five English ships arrived in Bermuda, each having a direct impact on the accounting of the Angolans taken from the *San Juan Bautista* and not left behind in Virginia. Initially, two vessels arrived, as documented by the Bermuda's *Shipping List*, which contains records of occasional visitors, emigrant vessels, magazine ships and private traders

Table 1: Ships to Arrive and Depart in Bermuda in the Fall of 1619/ Winter of 1620

Arrival[1]		Ship
1619	Aug.	A "barge," Captain Kerby arrives from the West Indies
1619	Aug.	Kerby reports meeting with a Dutch frigate with fourteen Africans from the *White Lion*
1619	Sept	The *Treasurer* arrived from Virginia
1619	Oct. 20	The *Warwick* arrived with Governor N. Butler; she was wrecked in a hurricane towards the end of November
1619	Nov.	The *Garland*, of 250 tons sent in June 1619 with 45 persons for Mr. John Farrar's plantation, Virginia, arrived 17 weeks out
1620	Jan.	The *Garland* returns to England with a cargo of tobacco.

---

[1] The arrival of Kerby's barge and the Dutch frigate is out of order as presented in the primary source document to align with the historical timeline as presented in the colonial records.

arriving at the Somers Island. The first was Captain Kerby's "barge" that exchanged victuals for fourteen Angolans. The next ship to arrive was the severely damaged *Treasurer*, with its share of twenty-nine Angolans stolen from the *San Juan Bautista*.[190]

The veracity of the actual number of Angolans on board is confirmed by a January 20, 1620 letter written to Lord Rich by John Dutton. In an account of his travels to Bermuda, he wrote:

> The Treasurer *arrived* [in Bermuda] *no longer seaworthy.* [That Captain] *Daniel Elfrith, after having done "some exploit (undoubtedly on the Spaniards)" had brought twenty-nine Africans, and some provisions from Virginia. There was a doubt about the right to the people and goods on the ship which had for this year been disposed of to the use of the Company. "It was Argall's unwonted boldness to his Lordship's name as a bolster to his unwarrantable actions." His Lordship had been "abused in the freight of his ship."*[191]

The second ship, which arrived on October 20, was the *Warwick*, named for its owner and one of the flagships of the Rich family shipping empire. The "300-ton vessel with a length on deck of about 30 meters to 34 meters" was on contract to the Virginia Company.[192] On this voyage, the ship was to bring passengers and supplies to Virginia. On its way to Virginia, it made a stop to bring the new governor of Bermuda, Captain Nathaniel Butler, to take command of the island as quickly as possible and replace the Earl of Warwick's nemesis, Miles Kendall.

The third ship to arrive in Bermuda was the *Garland*. During its Atlantic crossing, about "seventeen weeks into her voyage," the *Garland*'s vulnerable passengers were so close to running out of fresh water "that a sickness bred amongst them," which resulted in the death of many passengers and sailors, including the ship's Captain Whitney.[193] Realizing the precarious situation on board his ship, the *Garland*'s interim captain, William Wye, decided to stop at Bermuda so that his passengers could recover; this stop also provided the ship's crew an opportunity to restock supplies and get fresh water before continuing the voyage to Virginia.[194]

Each of the three ships that arrived on the island in the October/November period had a direct impact on the remaining original thirty or so Angolans taken from the *San Juan Bautista* not originally left behind in Virginia and eventually taken to Bermuda.

Within weeks, two major hurricanes struck the small English island, each with its own devastating consequences. The first of the two storms forced the *Garland* and the *Warwick* to take cover in Castle Harbor. Several weeks later, a second hurricane hit the island. The severe winds and rough seas of the second storm brutally battered the *Warwick* until it broke from its anchor, causing it to crash "against shallow reefs and sharp limestone cliffs…damaging its hull" and sink in Castle Harbor.[195] In 1979, a salvage expedition of the *Warwick* discovered that the ship was laden with heavy armor, suggesting that its real purpose on the voyage was more than just a supply vessel bringing needed provisions to the colonists—it was fitted more for acts of privateering.[196]

Having left its passengers in Virginia and reprovisioned and changed its cargo, the *Warwick* was to return to Bermuda and directed to transport the colony's end-of-season tobacco to England. However, once the *Warwick* sank from the hurricane, in order to make sure that the Bermuda tobacco got to market in England, Governor Butler instructed that the *Garland* be "refitted with materials taken from the *Warwick* which had foundered there." Then, the captain of the *Garland* was to alter the vessel's intended course to Virginia and take the tobacco to England instead.[197]

Governor Butler needed to find an alternative passage for the now stranded *Garland* passengers to get to their intended destination—Virginia—once they were rested and healthier.[198] Butler also wanted to get rid of the problematic Angolans as instructed by the Earl of Warwick before representatives from the Privy Council arrived to interview them and ask the critical questions pertinent to their actual arrival in Bermuda. The Pory and Rolfe letters essentially connected the dots for the Privy Council, filling in the gaps of the *when* and the *how* but leaving the open question of the *who*. Who was involved in the conspiracy? The testimony of the Angolans would be able to implicate many of London's prominent citizens.

Governor Nathaniel Butler wrote to the Earl of Warwick on October 9, 1620, that the Angolans had been "'disposed of,' according to directions."[199] While we still don't know the actual ship that brought the returning Angolans along with a number of the stranded *Garland* passengers to Virginia, Governor Butler was able to resolve two immediate problems. This strategic move benefited Butler, for he was already low on food and supplies for his own people in Bermuda and saw the chance to send the *Garland* passengers to John Ferrar, who intended to use them as headrights. Thus, Butler was able to reduce the risk of having the Angolans from the *San Juan Bautista* testify against Captain Elfrith, which would tie him and the Earl of Warwick to the piracy of the Spanish ship. Governor Butler was successful on all accounts. The clues to his success lie in three separate musters that were subsequently taken in Virginia in 1620, in 1623 and in 1624.

When John Rolfe wrote in his letter to Sir Edwin Sandys, he stated that there were "20 and Odd" Africans who arrived on the *White Lion*. Knowing that there were fourteen Angolans at Fleur de Hundred and an odd number dispersed throughout the colony is probably how Rolfe arrived at that number. However, several months later, a census was taken that listed thirty-two Angolans. Known as the 1620 Virginia Muster, the definitive number of fifteen males and seventeen females, has been universally accepted by historians as the accurate number of Africans in the Virginia colony. The number thirty-two would be roughly consistent with the number of Angolans traded for victuals by the *White Lion* and the number of Angolans left behind by the *Treasurer*.

In Lyon Gardiner Tyler's account, sixty Angolans were taken from the *San Juan Bautista*, and the number was roughly split between the two English ships.[200] The number of Angolans who disembarked from the *White Lion* in Virginia would have been that vessel's share of the thirty.

If the number of two or three Angolans left behind by the *Treasurer* on August 29, 1619, is accurate, as in a court disposition of John Wood, then this would account for the total number of thirty-two Africans, listed as "Non-Christians in the Service of the English" in the 1620 Census.[201]

In his letter to Edwin Sandys, Rolfe stated that Governor Yeardley and his cape merchant Abraham Piersey took the Angolans to their plantations. As evidenced by their actions, Yeardley and Piersey saw their powerful positions within the colony as vehicles for personal gain. By taking the lion's share of the Angolans, the two men in desperate need of workers ensured themselves the rewards of the Angolans' labor. According to the 1623 census, there were six Angolans residing at Governor George Yeardley's newly acquired one-thousand-acre plantation, Flowerdew, located on the lower portion of the James River, and an additional two were placed at his townhome in Jamestown. There were another six Angolans residing at Abraham Piersey's plantation, called Piersey Tolle, located on the Appomattox River.

It is doubtful that Governor Yeardley, who was aligned with the Virginia Company's treasurer, Sir Edwin Sandys, would have sent any of the Angolans taken from the *White Lion* in any large number to any of the men associated with former Governor Argall or with the Earl of Warwick, for fear of retribution from his sponsor Sir Edwin Sandys, his supporters or any of the members of the London Company. By keeping a disproportionate number of Angolans at Flowerdew and Piersey Tolle, Yeardley and Piersey increased their wealth by the Angolans' labor, exerted their control over the colony and minimized the benefit to the other landowners.

The subsequent census from February 16, 1623, listed five Angolans, who were mustered at Warrosquoke (also known as Warwick's Squeak or Bennett's Welcome), located on the lower side of the James River. Two of the Angolans were listed in the muster as servants at the residence of Puritan Edward Bennett. They were Antonio (later to be known as Anthony Johnson), who arrived on the *James* in 1621, and Maria (later to be known as Mary Johnson), who arrived on the *Margaret and John* in 1622.

Neither Antonio nor Maria could have physically been included in the 1620 census, for they hadn't arrived in Virginia by the date of the census, and the land they lived on, patented by Edward Bennett, a London merchant, was not patented until 1621 and populated between January and February 1622.

Author Tim Hashaw presents a plausible argument that there were Angolans located at the Bennett and Ewen plantations, suggesting that they were originally on the *Treasurer* and left for Bermuda only to return to Virginia months later:

> *The presence in 1623 of a half dozen Africans at Warrosquoke, Virginia, with the Latin names Francisco and Antonio imply they were either delivered by the* Treasurer *in 1619, or that were first taken to Bermuda after the* Bautista *attack and then shipped by Butler to England in 1621 and later shipped by Lord Rich to Virginia at different times. Warrosquoke was originally settled by Lord Rich's allies and business associates, including*

Francis West and the Puritans Edward Bennett and Richard Wiseman, who placed over six hundred immigrants there. The enmity between Lord Rich and Edwin Sandys, Miles Kendal and George Yeardley makes it unlikely that the Africans at Warrosquoke were from among the "20 and Odd" Bantu acquired by Yeardley and Piersey in late August 1619. Furthermore, both Yeardley and Piersey placed all of those Africans on their own private and public lands and did not trade them to other planters.[202]

While some of the Angolans from the *Treasurer* were sent to Virginia, an undetermined number of Angolans were also sent to the Earl of Warwick's impressive estate of Leighs Prior in Felsted, England. They became part of a colloquial "Bermuda Triangle" in that they arrived in Virginia from the Bay Campeche, only to remain on board the *Treasurer* before the ship holding them hastily escaped to Bermuda; then, in order to not be present to testify before the King's Privy Council, they were sent to England in exile; then, to ensure that they would be inaccessible to the Privy Council in England, they were shipped back to Virginia as part of the plot to conceal evidence from King James.

The Angolans dispatched to England from the *San Juan Bautista* were sent back to the Virginia colony on three different vessels. Antonio arrived in Virginia in 1621, on board the *James*; Maria arrived in 1622 on board the *Margaret and John*; and a young man named John Geaween (to be known as Graweere and then Gowen) arrived in 1622 on another voyage of the *James*. The fourth Angolan, Juan Pedro, first came on the *Discovery* in 1621 to New England, and then he finally arrived in Virginia in 1623 on board the *Swan*. These four particular Angolans' experiences were unique and substantially documented in the colonial records.[203]

Because these particular Angolans did not settle in the Virginia colony until after 1620, they could not have been counted in the colony's first muster, but each was included in the Muster of 1624–1625. As such, they could not have been part of the fourteen Angolans sent back to Virginia in late 1619 or early 1620.

Until 1622, the number of Africans remained relatively unchanged, since there was little importation of additional Africans. However, events in 1622 would cause another, more detailed census to be taken that provided more insight as to who these "20 and Odd" Africans, as alleged by John Rolfe, actually were and where they were distributed. The 1622 census would shed some light on the living conditions and circumstances of English America's first Africans.

From the first arrival of the English in Virginia, there were complications not only between Europeans and the Angolans, but also between the Indigenous American Powhatan Confederacy and the English, a relationship that was always tenuous at best. Captain Samuel Argall kidnapping Pocahontas, the daughter of the chief of the Powhatan, further increased this tension, and her subsequent marriage to John Rolfe only brought the two races to a briefly amicable relationship. While the release and marriage of Pocahontas brought the already strained relations to a temporary détente, this action may be considered the first of a long series of events that led directly to the quick decline of Powhatan's authority and the equally rapid rise of his brother Opechancanough's fortunes, culminating in the tragic Massacre of 1622.[204]

The long-stirring tensions between the white settlers and the Powhatans erupted on March 22, 1622, when Chief Opechancanough launched a surprise coordinated attack throughout the entire English colony. Plantations throughout the colony were attacked and set ablaze. The massacre was devastating. At Governor George Yeardley's Flowerdew Hundred Plantation, located on the south side of the James River, there were 6 deaths; at Captain Edward Bennett's plantation, there were 46; at Captain Berkeley's plantation, 27; within the Warrascoyack (Warrosquoke) patent, 7; and at Martin's Hundred, seven miles from James City, over 70 residents were killed, resulting in the staggering deaths of 347 men, woman and children, roughly a third of the colony's population.[205]

Having killed as many English as possible, the Indigenous Americans spared many of the Angolans or took them as captives. The African enslaved were taken to various native communities and then gradually integrated into the general population. Whether early Africans were captured by the Powhatans or escaped from the plantations where they lived, the Africans' introduction into the native population began the eventual slow integration of the African and Indigenous American races. From these early unions came the ancestors of present-day Americans of African descent.

Once the full impact of the attacks was realized, the colonists immediately took aggressive measures in their revenge against Opechancanough and his men. They first took steps to reduce Chief Opechancanough's sphere of influence and control over the area with a strong military attack on local Indigenous American villages, intending to reduce the number of villagers living in the area and to send the inhabitants fleeing. Continuing their retribution, the colonists then sent squads out looking to catch and assassinate Opechancanough. The attack ignited the Second Powhatan War.

When news of the attack reached England, it reverberated loudly throughout the kingdom. The Virginia Company immediately sent reinforcements and much-needed supplies to the colony. Infuriated by the news of the events, King James I summoned his Privy Council to seek advice on the next logical steps. Frustrated by the constant betrayal of English corsairs in privateering and now further incensed by the horrific massacre of his subjects in America, King James I required a full accounting of all of the inhabitants in the colony.

In the late spring of 1622, Edwin Sandys, treasurer of the Virginia colony, sent a letter informing the authorities that 347 people had been killed. Immediate action was initiated by John Ferrar on behalf of the Virginia Company of London by publishing the list of those slain, "To the end that their lawful heirs may take speedy order for their inheriting of their lands and estates there: For which the Honorable Company of Virgin are ready to do them all right and favor."[206]

Responding to the growing concerns over the events in the Virginia colony, the Privy Council set up a commission to investigate the conditions in Virginia and the management and finances of the Virginia Company. The king's detailed report, *A Declaration of the State of the Colony and Affairs of Virginia*, written by Edward Waterhouse, secretary to the Virginia Company of London, provided a firsthand account of the terror inflicted upon the colonists.[207]

The Massacre of 1622 had a profound effect on the colonists, and Waterhouse's *Declaration of the State* provided them with a spokesperson. The settlers "felt that this violent resistance by the native population liberated them from the constraints of their original moral justification for their occupation, that of 'civilizing' the indigenous population."[208] The massacre also had a profound effect on the Virginia Company of London; its investors now realized that the cost of running the colony was exorbitant and that there was unlikely to be any return on their investments. They were certain that the king was going to abolish their charter, and they were right in their assumption.

In order to ascertain the number of fatalities from the massacre, King James I ordered that a census be taken of the living and the dead; it is from this census that we begin to learn the location of where the *San Juan Bautista* Angolans lived and their identities.

Once King James I ascertained the true number of casualties in America, the massacre afforded the king "the plausible pretext for annulling the company's charter on the grounds of mismanagement."[209] After the

Table 1: 1623 Muster: *San Juan Bautista* Angolan Inhabitants
Living in Virginia, February 16, 1623[1]

	Identified on Muster (*No Last Name Provided*)	Muster of:	Census Location
1.	Unnamed Man	Gov. George Yeardley	Fleur de Hundred
2.	Unnamed Man	Gov. George Yeardley	Fleur de Hundred
3.	Unnamed Man	Gov. George Yeardley	Fleur de Hundred
4.	Unnamed Woman	Gov. George Yeardley	Fleur de Hundred
5.	Unnamed Woman	Gov. George Yeardley	Fleur de Hundred
6.	Unnamed Woman	Gov. George Yeardley	Fleur de Hundred
7.	Anthony	Abraham Piersey	Fleur de Hundred
8.	William	Abraham Piersey	Fleur de Hundred
9.	John	Abraham Piersey	Fleur de Hundred
10.	Anthony	Abraham Piersey	Fleur de Hundred
11.	Unnamed Female	Abraham Piersey	Fleur de Hundred
12.	Unnamed Female	Gov. George Yeardley	James City
13.	Unnamed Female	Gov. George Yeardley	James City
14.	Angelo	Captain William Pierce	James City
15.	Edward	Richard Kingsmill	Neck of Land
16.	John (Jiro)	Capt. Samuel Mathews	Near James City
17.	Anthony	Capt. Edward Bennett	Warwick Squrake
18.	Mary	Capt. Edward Bennett	Warwick Squrake
19.	Margaret	Capt. Edward Bennett	Warwick Squrake
20.	Frances	Capt. Edward Bennett	Warwick Squrake
21.	Peter	Capt. Edward Bennett	Warwick Squrake
22.	Antonio	Capt. William Tucker	Elizabeth City
23.	Isabell	Capt. William Tucker	Elizabeth City

---

[1] The 1623 Muster contains six unidentified Angolans who lived at living at the recently sold plantation of Governor Yeardley to Abrahm Piersey. The Angolans are now under contract to Dr. John Woodson, now living at Fleur de Hundred, see HOT: *Original Lists of Persons of Quality*. p. 169-189.

incidents surrounding the pirating of the *San Juan Bautista* and the charges from the Spanish ambassador, the king and his advisors had assumed for some time that the dereliction of duty of the Virginia Company's officers and shareholders, the company's mismanagement and the infighting, which was believed to have contributed to the horror in the colony, would culminate in the dissolution of the charter. The massacre had finally set into motion King James's inevitable termination of the charter in June 1624; he then assumed responsibility for the colony's management. King James set in motion the establishment of a royal council in England and a royal governor and council in Virginia.[210]

As the first royal governor, Sir Francis Wyatt was retained by King James and commissioned a new muster under the royal charter. The muster, taken from January 20 through February 7, 1625, reported that the colony's

Table 1: 1623 Muster: *San Juan Bautista* African Inhabitants
Deceased in Virginia, February 16, 1623[1]

Identified on Muster	Muster of:	Census Location
Unknown	Capt. Samuel Mathews	Sherlow Hundred

[1] Ibid.

population consisted of 1,232 inhabitants. The census listed 23 Angolans and 1 Indigenous American, all reported as servants. They lived on seven plantations scattered from the mouth of the James River to Flowerdew Hundred. From this muster we can now begin to construct who the previously unidentified Angolans were on board the *San Juan Bautista*, before arriving in the Virginia colony in 1619.[211] In 1902, James Curtis Ballagh wrote in *A History of Slavery in Virginia*:

> *From a careful comparison of these lists with documents showing the location of these planters and their plantations in 1623 and 1625, respectively, it seems certain that the persons in possession of the [Angolans] were the same in both years, and doubtless had had control of them from their first introduction in 1619, 1621 and 1623. There is nothing to suggest that a single transfer of possession had taken place after being fixed, though in several cases the [Angolans] had been moved from one place or plantation to another by their possessors. Not more than three instances of this even seem to have occurred: three women were removed probably from Governor Yeardley's [plantation] to his place in Jamestown; a child and his mother…were transferred from Warrasqueak to Abraham Piercey's estate, called Piercey Hundred; John a body-servant, probably of Captain West's, accompanied him…from James City to Elizabeth City."[212]*

The Muster of 1624–1625, commissioned by King James, was a detailed house-to-house survey that contained information about the locations of widely dispersed households in the Virginia colony, as well as information about relationships between people who lived in these households. The relationships in the various households are a critical piece of information for contemporary scholars of African American history as they provide information on the number of servants in certain households and the number and gender of the Angolans in residence.

As provided by the musters of 1624 and 1625, we find the records of the first true distribution of the Angolans from the *San Juan Bautista* and where within the colony they lived. As a result of the primary names of the households recorded in the muster, we learn that the charter generation Angolans were distributed between six households. In three of the households, fifteen of the Angolans (65.2 percent) are found, and the remaining eight are found in five additional households. It is within these households that the Angolans who were originally on board the *San Juan Bautista* and eventually arrived in the Virginia colony have been identified.

In each of the households where Angolans were listed, there were also European indentured servants living on the property. In extrapolating the more detailed information from these first census records, we can actually begin to identify some of the original Angolans by their primary and surnames and, more importantly, by their African birth names.

The Angolans had Christian names, and while such names could easily be explained as being given to them by the English, they were not English names. The Angolans had names that were deep-rooted in the Catholic Church of central Africa, and were, in Spanish and Portuguese, indicative of the region of Ndongo in which they were born and from where they came.[213] In keeping with the practice of Iberian Catholics, Christian names in central Africa were taken from the names of the Catholic saints. From the sixteenth century onward, virtually all Kongolese had saints' names, and even non-Christians in Angola sometimes bore these names.[214] Translated from Latin

Table 1: Distribution of Servants in Virginia, 1625[1]

Muster	Total No. of Servants	Africans[2]			
		Male	Female	Child	Total
G. Yeardley	36	3	5	0	8
A. Piersey	40	4	2	1	7
W. Tucker	18	1	1	1	3
W. Pierce	17	0	1	0	1
E. Bennett	12	1	1	0	2
F. West	6	1	0	0	1
R. Kingsmill*	4	1	0	0	1
Total	133	11	10	2	23

[1] Hecht, Irene, "The Virginia Muster of 1624/5 As a Source for Demographic History," *The W&MQ*, Third Series, Vol. 30, No. 1 (1973), p. 78.
[2] It appears that several Angolans, particularly Margaret who resided on the John Chew plantation, and a John who arrived on board the James in 1622, and a Michael and Katherine who resided on the William Ewen plantation were not included in the Muster. Although William Ewen spent long period of time in the Virginia colony, his permanent residence was in Kent, England. For many of the absentee landowners, if they were not present at the time of the muster, no information was provided relative to the inhabitants on the plantation.

into Portuguese, these included such common names as João, Francisco, Pedro, Manuel, Simão, Miguel, Antonio, Matteo and Bernardo, as well as less common ones like Jeronimo, Sylvester, Abel and Lourenço. Women also had a wide range of Christian names from the Iberian Peninsula: Maria, Joana, Isabela, Luisa, Ana and Graça joined with more exotic names such as Cecilia, Martha, Eva and Virginia.[215]

One of the county's leading planters and the commander of Point Comfort was Captain William Tucker, who lived in the shire then known as Elizabeth City (present-day city of Hampton). He acquired two Angolans, a man identified as "Antonio" and a woman identified as "Isabella." According to the detailed Muster of 1624–1625, there were only twenty-three Angolans listed in the Virginia colony.[216] The reduction of the number of Angolans in the colony can probably be attributed to the escape of Angolans friendly with the local Indigenous American tribesmen, who probably ran off with their oppressed kindred spirits during the 1622 Massacre—or they were captured or died of natural causes.[217] In 1624, according to the List of the Inhabitants, Antony and Isabella had an infant, likely the first Angolan child to be baptized, whom they named William, presumably after Captain William Tucker.[218]

As will be discussed later, many of the Angolans from the *San Juan Bautista* worked in the fields side by side with the newly arrived white indentured servants in the same condition of servitude, indicating for most that their servitude was temporary. Thus, such temporary servitude could very well be distinguished from slavery.

In order to determine if these Angolans in particular were treated by their masters the same as the European indentured servants, ultimately receiving their independence within an established period of time, a careful examination of known Africans and their status within the households or properties where they lived, as well as their experiences in the preceding years, will provide tremendous insight as to whether they became enslaved or became free people of color.

When the Angolans originally left Africa, they undoubtedly were intended to be sold in Vera Cruz, New Spain. The narrow window of time during which they arrived in Virginia, along with the unique chain of events and circumstances surrounding their arrival and settlement in the colony, has caused much speculation in American history on whether or not these particular African men, women and children were ever enslaved people or only indentured servants.

At the time of the Africans' arrival at Point Comfort, the Virginia Company of London and its colony had no legal precedent for the arrival of the Angolans. The Virginia Company, operating under English Common Law, had only two classifications for settlers in the colony—freeman and indentured servant. The Virginia colony was for all intents and purposes a "company town" where everything and everyone belonged to the Virginia Company of London.

However, there was no contractual relationship in Luanda, Angola, for the sale or purchase of these displaced Angolans between the Virginia Company of London or any of the landowners in the Virginia colony. The captured Spanish/Portuguese enslaved Angolans were pirated—they were stolen, and by virtue of the illegal piracy of the *San Juan Bautista*, the Angolans still legally belonged to the Spanish crown. Once the Angolans from the *San Juan Bautista* arrived, they were divided between two of the most prominent men in the colony, the governor and his cape merchant, neither of whom had any legal rights to the enslaved.

As the Angolans were in a state of limbo in terms of their legal status within the colony, they may have benefited from the indentured servant system established by the Virginia Company, as well as the newly established headright system offered to those who could afford to pay the passage of laborers to the colony.

The act of piracy that brought the Angolans to the colony only fueled the longstanding bitter animosity between the Virginia Company investors and similar rivalries within the colony. It was from these open hostilities between the investors in London and their acrimonious residual effects in the colonial outposts of Virginia that the Angolans from the *San Juan Bautista* may have benefited.

Upon arrival in 1619, in every measurable way possible, conditions in Virginia were deplorable. For the English peasant class, working in America was hard and, for many, had life-threatening consequences. Their work hours were long, the food was scarce, disease was rampant and they were the ones working in the fields when the Indigenous Americans attacked, leaving them within striking distance of a well-targeted arrow shot in their direction. Meanwhile, the landed gentry in the colony and their investors in London looked for ways to enhance their fortunes at every turn possible and to squeeze as much profit out of their poor countrymen.

For additional profits, the English privateers looked to the rivers and tributaries of the Chesapeake Bay. The abundant waterways and hidden coves provided substantial cover for the potential illicit acts of piracy that the wealthy English "gentlemen" desired and engaged in to fill their personal coffers with pirated goods. Several of the investors of the Virginia Company and their cohorts within the colony chose this as a viable but illegal option to enrich themselves. A secondary objective was to smuggle in desperately needed supplies not provided by the investors back in England to the settlers in order to buy their silence. Some of the growing influential sea captains of the colony, such as Governor Yeardley and Captain Pierce, built impressive homes on Jamestown Island along the secluded deep creek canal that divided the back side of the island. They further enriched themselves by smuggling goods and people to the docks nestled behind their homes. It is now believed that it was on this deep creek that the Angolans who were originally on the *Treasurer*—those who were brought to Bermuda before returning to the Virginia colony—arrived.

When Europeans first went to Africa, they witnessed how Africans enslaved their captured enemies. Slavery was not a new concept to the Angolans, particularly those from the noble and merchant classes. However, the enslaved were traditionally prisoners of war and/or of the lower classes and often assimilated over time. In their 1618–19 attack of the capital city of Kabasa, the Portuguese enslaved members of the Angolan nobility and merchant class, which was more unique—and treacherous. Once in America, these same Africans understood the importance of protecting their own legal rights as nonenslaved people. In 1625, a new arrival to the colony took extraordinary measures to protect himself from being in perpetual bondage, thereby beginning to define the early role of Africans in Virginia.

7

A COLONY OF INDENTURES AND HEADRIGHTS

After Powhatan's Massacre of 1622 and the disbanding of the London Virginia Company's charter, the fortunes for Virginia's land barons improved dramatically. Once the colony and its land barons began to generate revenue from tobacco, the ruthlessness of the colony's elite became more pronounced. While Virginia was still frontier land, "it passed increasingly into the hands of small, but self-serving immigrant elite." The men who ruled the colony were not the Virginia gentlemen portrayed in our nation's history books or romance novels but a group of self-serving and cutthroat Machiavellis who believed the ends justified the means. "One of the richest of them was Captain Abraham Piersey, who ran the company store and sold provisions to other immigrants at three times the set price. His books always showed a loss, yet he grew from 'a very poor man' to the richest leader in the colony, with forty servants in 1625," including seven Angolans from the *San Juan Bautista*.[219]

After the Powhatan Massacre, Captain Piersey, along with other captains who were veterans of the Anglo-Spanish War, was emboldened to use any means necessary to maintain power and to amass fortune. After Piersey, "the next most affluent master, with thirty-six servants in 1625," including eight Angolans from the *San Juan Bautista*, was Governor George Yeardley, "a right worthy statesmen for his own profit," as one Virginian bitterly described him. Yeardley arrived with "nothing more valuable than a sword," made a fortune by "notable impressions, looted the colony and went back to London with fourteen servants in livery." Another ship captain whose ruthlessness demonstrated the ends to which each man would go was William Tucker, "who won the company's commission to trade with the Indigenous Americans." Still angered over the 1622 Massacre, in retaliation, "when the Pamunkey Americans threatened his business, he invited 200 to a feast and murdered them all with poisoned wine; those slow to die were beheaded."[220]

Shortly after King James I suspended the Virginia Company's charter in 1624, he died. At the time of his death, England's urban centers were under tremendous pressure from overcrowding, unemployment, blight and disease. James I was succeeded by his son Charles I. To relieve the pressure on England's inner cities, the newly crowned king decided it was in his best interest to aggressively advance the headright system in the Virginia colony.

Fulfilling the headright needs in Virginia benefited England and the new king in a number of ways, including a reduction of political pressures at home by curtailing the urban population. An increase in new immigrants in America allowed the Crown to solidify its hold in America and its presence worldwide, and the additional laborers in Virginia permitted the colony to produce more tobacco and helped fill the coffers of the monarchy. However, the rapid growth of the headright system in Virginia also solidified the deepening divide in the colony's burgeoning caste system and exerted tremendous pressure on the colony's governance.

As tobacco became an important cash crop for the colony, money began to flow in Virginia and into coffers back in England. On January 6, 1630, King Charles I passed a law requiring all tobacco imported into England to be grown in the American colonies. His proclamation further stipulated that imported tobacco could not be grown in any of the English isles or any other European colonies. The increasing revenue base from taxes on the tobacco served as a major incentive for the king's decision. Any trepidation the king had about the increasing indentured population in the Virginia colony quickly became secondary to the rising tax base to the royal treasury.

Virginia's royalist planters benefited from the king's tobacco monopoly, and Governor Yeardley helped guide the transformation of Virginia into a royal colony. In return, England provided those known as the "great planters" of the colony with a steady supply of inexpensive labor from its urban poor. As the great planters expanded their land holdings, they held the belief that Indigenous Americans in Virginia were not Christians. The English, as well as the Spanish and Portuguese before them, held that they had God-given, inalienable rights to the land they "discovered" in America.

Once in Virginia, the English entered into various battles with the neighboring Indigenous American tribes and then would enter treaties with

King James I called smoking a "filthy novelty," but tobacco proved the salvation of his Virginia colony. Seeds from the West Indies, grown in Virginia's soil and climate, produced a pleasing leaf. From 1615 to 1619, tobacco exports increased twentyfold. *Courtesy U.S. National Park Service; Sidney E. King Collection.*

them that expanded their rights to additional land holdings. The abundant land in America enabled the English, who left feudal land aristocracy, to bring their own concepts of land ownership, class relations and the privileges flowing from inheritance.

For the land barons, in order to expand their wealth, for every indenture contract that could be proven, the owner of the indenture was awarded a land grant or patent for a headright, which consisted of a fifty-acre tract of land. The headright system paved the way for additional colonial expansion into undeveloped lands. It was also a valuable vehicle to obtain both land and the necessary laborers to develop the land and to build continued wealth and power. To benefit more from this system, early Virginians would also use the Angolans by transporting them as potential workers—thus counting them as headrights—in order to acquire more land rights. This system benefited both the holder of the patent and any savvy indenture, white or black, who negotiated some form of payment in turn for acquiring their own land, as evidenced by several of the Angolans in future years.

In order to receive a headright, the sponsor of the headright had to obtain a patent for the land. The sponsor would provide the name of the individual(s) who was sponsored to be imported into the colony and a description and a survey of the land to ensure that it did not infringe on any other owner's land rights. According to Yale history professor and expert on colonial headrights Edmund S. Morgan:

There were several stages in obtaining a patent for land by use of headrights. First, it was necessary to get a certificate, either from the governor and council or from a county court, testifying to the importation of the persons for whom the rights were claimed. With the certificate in hand, the claimant had an official survey made of the land he wanted (the survey might consist of little more than the description). He then went to the secretary of the colony, who made out the patent, usually copying it from the certificate the names of the person transported. Finally the governor signed or sealed the document. Patents were recorded by the secretary. County courts seem to have been haphazard about recording the certificates they issued, but they did record many of them.[221]

The headright system developed into a well-established feudal caste system that perpetuated the wealth for landowners, who acquired poor whites from England to farm the land as cheaply as possible, allowing the landowners to maximize profits. The massive accumulation of headrights and thereby land ownership among a few powerful individuals created influential and wealthy oligarchies within the Virginia colony.

From the beginning of the colony in 1607 until the arrival of the Angolans from the *San Juan Bautista* in 1619, Virginia was overwhelmingly populated by white indentured servants in their "early twenties, and eighty to ninety percent were male."[222] From the very beginning, the large number of men arriving in the colony concerned the kingdom of Spain. In fact, from the founding of the Virginia colony, England had misled Spain, whose monarchy believed Virginia was to be nothing more than a penal colony to warehouse the most hardened criminals, rather than a colony for expansive development and settlement.

According to noted colonial historian Peter Wilson Coldham, Spain, "being suspicious of England's intentions in the New World, sought advice from its Embassy in London." Ambassador to the Court of Saint James, Diego Sarmiento de Acuña, Count of Gondomar, replied, "Their [the English's] principle reason for colonization is to give an outlet to so many idle and wretched people as they have in England."[223] The sundry group of men who came to Virginia included men who were convicts or had commuted sentences:

Between 1614 and 1775, amounting to some 50,000 men, women and children, all but an insignificant minority belonging to the poorest class and most were sentenced for crimes which today might incur a small fine or, more likely, probation. Roughly half of all those sold into American slavery were sentenced by the courts in and around London which, throughout its history, has acted as a magnet to the poor, the idle, the shiftless and the ambitious.[224]

The erroneous belief that the first documented Angolans arriving in Virginia had to be slaves since they didn't have indenture contracts fails to understand that there were a multitude of reasons for European foreigners to come to Virginia, voluntarily or involuntarily. Similar to the ubiquitous legal condition of the Angolans, not all of the English who arrived in the colony had indenture contracts. Convicts and those with commuted sentences, as well as unaccompanied minors, arrived in the colony without indenture contracts. There were also those who, for unscrupulous reasons, were kidnapped and brought aboard transport ships that needed to fill their quota for laborers to be sent to America. It has been generally summarized that the indentured servants

were traditionally viewed as socially marginal individuals....Many were convicts from jails, transported instead of being hanged; a few were political and military prisoners taken in war or rebellion. They were rogues, vagabonds, whores, cheats, and rabble of all descriptions raked from the gutter and kicked out of the country.[225]

While the conditions and social status of the above were quite different from the conditions of the Africans who arrived in America, when the Angolans from the *San Juan Bautista* arrived in the Virginia colony, the issue of servitude without contract was not a situation unique to the Angolans. This issue of servitude without a contract was such a wide-scale problem that it was debated in the 1642 and again in the 1654 General Assemblies, though neither addressed the conditions of the Angolans but instead discussed the conditions of European laborers without an indenture contract.

At the 1642 General Assembly, the legislators recognized that within the colony, there were those in servitude working in a *quantum meritus* status, for whatever reason, without contract. The matter created such tension within the colony that during the legislative session, the Virginia Assembly defined the terms and the length of servitude depending on the age of the indentured servant:

WHEREAS many controversies have risen between masters and servants being brought into the colony without indentures or covenants to testify their agreements whereby both masters and servants have been often prejudiced, Be it therefore enacted and confirmed for prevention of future controversies of the like nature, that such servants as shall be imported having no indentures or covenants either men or women if they be above twenty year old to serve four years, if they shall be above twelve and under twenty to serve five years, And if under twelve to serve seven years.[226]

The issue of indenture without a contract arose prominently as the colony's caste system became more pronounced. As more of England's poor came to Virginia to work in the fields, the separation of class became more distinct. The great planters bought and sold their servants, white and black, without regard to English law:

Thomas Best in 1623 complained that his master "hath sold me for £150 sterling like a damn slave." A few brave souls challenged the elite and as a result suffered the results by becoming victimized by their masters. When Richard Crocker complained that Piersey "dealt upon nothing but extortion," the plaintiff had his ears nailed to the pillory. Richard Barnes in 1624 was sentenced to have his arm broken and his tongue bored through with an awl. He was then made to run a gauntlet of forty men and was butted by every one of them and then "kicked downe and footed out of the fort." Others were executed for lesser offenses.[227]

As the tobacco industry grew, the need for men in the colony also grew. The hard work needed to grow the crop turned the colony into a bastion of single men. According to historian Edmund S. Morgan, professor at Yale University and past president of the Organization of American Historians, "immigration in the seventeenth century was predominantly male."

In his analysis of the colony's 1625 census, Morgan found that "Virginia had a sex ratio of 333 men to 100 women, and miscellaneous evidence argues that immigration tended to sustain the imbalance." Further evidence suggests in cross reference that if the record of headrights awarded is accurate, "they tell much of the same story."[228] In Professor Morgan's analysis, the population of the Virginia colony was concentrated between sixteen and thirty-five years of age, during which most women are in their child-bearing years.

The disproportionate number of men to women raised serious concerns for the colonial leaders, particularly as the young men began to seek out short- and long-term relationships with Indigenous American women. It

Table 1: Ages Given for 750 Persons out of 1,210
Living in January and February, 1625[1]

Age	Male	Female	Total
1-5	30	23	53
6-9	5	9	14
10-15	41	10	51
16-19	81	4	85
20-24	212	32	244
25-29	106	14	120
30-34	65	11	76
35-39	41	5	46
Over 39	53	8	61
Total	634	116	750

---

[1]   Ibid, 408.

was only a matter of time before the men would also seek out consensual relationships with African women or sexually assault them outright. Such measures did not go unnoticed.

As an example, on September 17, 1630, an Englishman was punished for being caught engaging in a sexual relationship with an African woman:

> *Hugh Davis was to be soundly whipped, before an assembly of Negroes and others for abusing himself to the dishonor of God and shame of Christians, by defiling his body in lying with a negro; which fault he is to acknowledge next Sabbath day.*[229]

Although then-governor George Yeardley and Sir Edwin Sandys had previously transported one hundred "maids, young and uncorrupt," to the colony, it still was not enough to make the colony "family-friendly" and self-populating. It was increasingly clear that the colony was becoming populated with interracial children, as English fathers moved in with and took non-English women as wives. From these early unions, we begin to see the first of many generations of mixed-race African children with English names.

Global colonization was an attractive concept, in part due to the restrictions imposed by European feudalism. For the investors in the Virginia Company and the English settlers in the Virginia colony, colonizing in America provided an opportunity to move out of the restrictive society of land ownership and feudal labor arrangements. The availability of "unclaimed" land in America was an attractive incentive to settle in the Virginia colony for investors, nobility, small landholders and the peasant class.

By 1634, the colony's population consisted of 4,914 settlers. As a result of the colony's progress and the growing challenges of managing the expanding Virginia colony from England, the recently crowned King Charles I established a new form of local government in the colony—the shires. Modeled after the English form of local government, each shire was managed by local supervisors called a shire (present-day sheriff). The shire was responsible for collecting taxes and fines, documenting land transactions and serving as the leading centralized law enforcement officer.

On April 19, 1638, Georg Mynifie (later to be spelled George Menefie), a wealthy landowner, took advantage of the headright system and increased his land holdings by importing Angolans and amassed over three thousand acres of land, serving as a model for other would-be land barons. According to the Abstracts of Virginia Land Patents and Grants, Mynifie, upon arriving in the colony from England, brought with him sixty headrights. His headright patent listed thirty-seven individuals, including indentured servants he brought from England with him.[230] In deducting the remaining number, the twenty-three Angolans became the first large lot imported directly from England and not from Africa or the Caribbean.

The administration of the headright system helped to quickly populate the shires of Virginia, which were Accomac, Charles City, Charles River Shire, Elizabeth City, Henrico, James City, Warwick River and Warrosquyoake.[231] All forms of local government within the shires were housed in a central location (county courthouses) and were to include documentation on all local transactions and legal matters, including information on land deeds, administrative or judicial orders and the last wills and testaments of the shires' residents.[232]

During the early and mid-seventeenth century in colonial Virginia, there were only two types of people: rich or poor. In populating the colony, the poor of England, who became indentured servants, left behind for historians and genealogists a rich paper trail of detailed indenture contracts. Since births, deaths and marriages were not recorded in the early years of the Virginia colony, the indentured contracts located in each of the eight shires enable scholars and historians to accurately capture information about inhabitants of the colony.

Information found in the courthouses of the shires included the names and other relevant details about the shires' inhabitants, which can be extrapolated from indenture contracts and the headright registers. These same colonial records also begin to provide a legal footprint of substantial information on the first documented Angolans and others as found in the county deed, orders and will books, often used today by genealogists and descendants.

Governor Yeardley's representative government, founded in 1619, a month before the arrival of the first documented Angolans, began to define itself legislatively. Although the colony followed English Common Law, it further defined the rules in which the colonists would govern themselves. The foundation of colonial law was based on an established complex legal system that provided the framework to mediate continuous disputes and to centralize dispute resolution. The legal system established common laws based on the legal principle of determining points in litigation according to precedent, known as *stare decisis*, where judges and courts would honor previous rulings as precedent.

As evidenced in the legal records, the first documented Africans were astute, quickly learned how to take advantage of the English legal system and can be found in the colonial records. According to historian Ira Berlin, the colony's African population:

> *Like their white neighbors…were a litigious people. Throughout the seventeenth century they sued and were sued with great frequency, testifying and petitioning as to their rights. Although many black men and women fell prey to the snares of Anglo-American jurisprudence—bastardy acts, tax forfeitures, and debt penalties—their failure was rarely one of ignorance, as members of the charter generations proved adept at challenging the law on its own terms and rarely abandoned a losing cause without appeal.*[233]

By 1635, in the land records, wealthy landowners began the formal practice of including in the headright system the names of Angolans along with the English who paid their admittance to the Virginia colony or their travel costs to a new colony or territory. Some former indentured servants, white and black, were able to buy out their own contracts or complete their contractual commitment and then were able to buy headrights for themselves.

EPILOGUE

On that hot humid day in August 1619, as Captain John Colyn Jope of the *White Lion* entered the still waters of the Chesapeake Bay, little did he know that he would be permanently changing the course of American history and the democratic principles on which the colony would be founded. The arrival of his cargo of 14 Angolans would become the most famous of the more than 350,000 men, women and children to arrive directly from Africa as part of the brutal but highly profitable transatlantic slave trade.

Four hundred years after the arrival of the first documented Africans in English North America, there continues to be a debate among historians about their legal status within the colony. The unintended consequences of their arrival in 1619 would set the stage half a century later for the introduction of laws codifying the institution of African slavery in the Virginia colony. These and subsequent laws have since become the origin of the history of Africans in North America, leading to the mistaken belief that the Angolans of the *San Juan Bautista* were enslaved when in fact that body of laws did not apply to their first fifty years in the colonies.

The evolution of Virginia's slave laws has become a dark stain on our nation's past and has tainted the legacy of our nation's founding fathers for their inability to address and end this "peculiar institution" during the Constitutional Convention in 1787.[234] The institution of slavery and all of its residual effects can still be felt today in every corner of American society, in our boardrooms, in our classrooms and the backrooms of legislative and judicial bodies all across the nation.

In 1607, when Captain Newport arrived in the Chesapeake Bay, the English invaded a land already known to the indigenous people as Tsenacommacah. He brought with him three ships with hundreds of "foreign aliens" to invade a land with their customs, their language and their laws. But these laws, only known by the "illegal foreigners" as English Common Law, had no provision for the enslavement of the indigenous people of Tsenacommacah or the enslavement of Africans who would arrive some twelve years later. However, a half century later, the English invaders would codify new laws that would incrementally create the institution of slavery, the antithesis of the democratic values espoused at Governor George Yeardley's conclave on July 30, 1619, where the first representative assembly in English America would forge the democratic principles upon which the nation would be founded. It would be within those same democratic principles that the first documented Africans of English North America litigated in the colonial courts of Virginia to protect and ensure their rights as indentured men or women as allowed to them by English Common Law.

Unlike their fellow captives from the African continent who would follow for the next two hundred years and were enslaved for perpetuity by laws enacted in the mid-seventeenth century, the *San Juan Bautista* Angolans arrived when England's poor were sold into servitude, albeit for a defined period of seven to twenty-five years.[235] Servitude contracts were bought and sold, and the servants bound by these contracts often went to court to litigate their release or the conditions under which they worked.

When the English came to Tsenacommacah in 1607, its objectives for invasion and subsequent colonization were in part to compete in world markets with its fierce adversaries, the Catholic monarchies of Spain and Portugal, as well as to dramatically reduce its surplus labor from all across the English landscape by exporting the poor to America. Unlike their adversaries from the Iberian Peninsula, the English colonizing America had little interest in enslaving the indigenous people of North America or importing enslaved people from Africa or elsewhere, as the English assumed they had the needed surplus labor force for colonization from within their own borders.

During this period, England was considered by its Catholic nemeses as a country steeped in protestant Calvinism, continuous inclement weather, limited natural resources and a landscape barely able to provide sufficient sustenance to feed its people due to its cold and damp climate and growing conditions, coupled with its medieval feudal management system in land management and farming.[236] During the period of King William the Conqueror in 1086, the king, desiring to know more about the topography and his people, commissioned a national survey of England, known by its works as the *Doomsday Book*. As little had changed from 1086 to the mid-sixteenth century, the national survey provides tremendous insight:

> *England consisted of arable land (35%), woodland (15%), pasture (30%), and meadow (1%); the rest was mountain and fen and heath and waste and wild. The manor (which was the linchpin of the social order of England) was the foundation of agrarian and economic life. The Lords land was known as "demesne" land; it might be adjacent to the manor house, or it might be scattered in strips among the fields. The free tenants paid him rent for their acreage and were obliged to help him at the busy times of harvest; on free tenants or villieins they performed weekly labor service and work such as threshing or winnowing. The terms of this labor were managed by tradition. Approximately 10% of the population were deemed to be held in slavery, while 14% were described as "freemen;" the rest of the population were part of a variable range between the two.[237]*

By the late 1400s, Spain and Portugal dominated the high seas. England had a slow start in international seafaring and at colonization and, by the late 1500s, understood that foreign colonies constituted the natural goal of all exploration and voyaging. The English were long frustrated in their attempts to emulate the colonial successes of the Spaniards, the Portuguese, the Dutch and the French.[238] In 1607, after being engaged in a nineteen-year war with Spain, England had rising debts and an unskilled labor force and was considered hundreds of years behind its more economically, socially and culturally advanced Catholic state adversaries.

While the Spanish union suffered from its own internal discord, including acts of rebellion within and outside of its borders, racial strife in its vast network of colonies and greed and corruption, its challenges paled to those of England. And it was within England's challenges that colonization in America would provide the ability to reduce its surplus labor pool before rebellion erupted internally. "In the century before 1640, [England's] population was growing faster than food resources, resulting in the occasional and localized food sort shortage so severe as to cause hunger, starvation and death."[239] In 1600, the total population of England was close to 4.1 million, and by the midcentury mark, the population had reached a peak of almost 5.3 million.[240] Although its population was only a quarter of the population of the Iberian Peninsula, England's internal economic, social and political rivalries had adverse consequences for the island nation.

By the early seventeenth century, about the time the first documented Africans arrived in Virginia, there was widespread unemployment in England. "Agriculture remained the major source of employment, but the work in the fields was seasonal and hundreds of thousands found the laboring sufficient for part but not all of the year," resulting in long-term chronic underemployment, a structural problem of too many part-time workers seeking full-time work.[241]

Due to the early exportation of the English poor to the colony in America, by the 1620s, "famine begins to disappear as a visible threat, supported by increased agricultural production, better communication and lines of credit, and the leveling off of its population [growth] dramatically solved some of England's problems."[242] With the establishment of a colony in Virginia, the export of its surplus labor aided in the gradual reduction of England's unemployed and as a result continued to be an objective for the remainder of the seventeenth century. Contrary to widespread beliefs, the introduction of African slave labor into the Virginia colony was not an objective or considered a desired outcome of the Virginia Company of London, for it barely had enough food to feed its English inhabitants, let alone additional and unexpected Africans or any other non-English group of laborers.

It's hard to fathom that escape from slavery was possible for any group of African men, women or children kidnapped from their family and homes, branded, enslaved, then transported to the Americas in the putrid bellies of slave ships. However, slavery would not become the fate of the *San Juan Bautista* Angolans. History has not been kind to the "20 and Odd" Angolans referenced by John Rolfe in his letter to Sir Edwin Sandys in 1620. As Americans, we have been so conditioned by what we were taught, the books we read and by the mass media that it is almost impossible to conceive of a period in which Africans in the English colony were in fact free people of color. We assume the only status the first Africans in English America and their descendants could have had was that of slaves, and by virtue the color of their skin, they must have been relegated to an inferior status within the colony and thereby American history.

In the early days of American mass media, fictionalized portrayals of those from the African continent were reductive and ill-informed; for example, in the oft-adapted story of Tarzan, an English boy who was raised in the jungles of Africa by gorillas (often the first fictional exposure for many to Africa as a continent and to its people), early depictions show the indigenous people of Africa having limited verbal skills and no developed language, only communicating in monosyllabic noises and grunts. The mass media version of Africans seemingly wore only grass skirts or loin cloths, dancing around a black steaming pot of boiling water, ostensibly prepared for some cannibalistic ritual of having a frightened Englishman for their next meal.

The old black-and-white televised versions of these stories are dimly lit, and the Africans are so dark in color that viewers could see only the whites of their eyes or their (usually bared) teeth. Even in the case of the fictionalized Tarzan's story, the gorillas that raised him are depicted as more articulate and intelligent than the Africans living on the continent. Although these stories suggest that these depictions were historically accurate, they reflect only a white supremacist false narrative perpetuated by eighteenth-century historians in an effort to subjugate and disenfranchise Africans.

Even today, while time and civil rights measures have passed, our media still strongly influences our perception of Africans; at the time of this publication, the most recent Tarzan adaptation was *The Legend of Tarzan*, which—while perhaps less overtly racist than earlier versions—still depicts black characters as less innately competent than white ones. As quoted in the *Los Angeles Times*, sociologist Matthew Hughey noted, "Tarzan is a time machine. He transports these 19th century views into the 20th and 21st centuries. He reassures audiences that down deep there is a natural order to things."[243] This belief in a "natural order" perpetuates the false belief that Africans must have been enslaved.

As documented by Diogo Cão in his extensive letters to officials in Portugal in 1483, the Africans with which he came into contact from Angola fit none of these stereotypes. It is through Diogo Cão's firsthand accounts that we learn that the indigenous people of the region of Africa where the *San Juan Bautista* Angolans originated were an advanced, permanently settled farming and herding people who forged iron tools and weapons and who lived in the same towns year-round.[244] The people of Angola had advanced verbal and communication skills and came from highly developed kingdoms similar to those of Western Europe. The Angolans who arrived in Virginia in 1619 after being forced on board the *San Juan Bautista* did not comport to the stereotypical African. But it is within this embedded stereotype that some present-day historians continue with the belief that the Angolans of the *San Juan Bautista* had to be enslaved or treated as slaves merely because of their nationality and/or the color of their skin.

When the first documented Angolans arrived in the colony, they found a fledging backwater settlement less advanced than their robust royal city of Kabasa, Angola. When the Angolans arrived, the leaders and founders of the settlement were experienced sea captains who had amassed substantial land holdings in the colony but were inexperienced in the trades of a land-based economy. The Virginia Company of London, which founded and funded the colony in North America, based its business model on making hefty profits for its shareholders and intended to use the cheapest labor force possible to maximize on the returns for its investors. The company sent its nation's poor to Virginia to work on the subdivided land under a plantation system as laborers under contractual indenture agreements. The newly transplanted indentured servants in Virginia had little to no experience in soil and agriculture and insufficient knowledge of animal husbandry or forest management—they lacked the basic skills that could have aided in the development of the newly established colony. Many were mere victims of the harsh realities of England's clearly defined medieval caste system, as the English laborers sent to America came from the lower economic and social spheres of England's feudal system. They were poorly educated, had little knowledge or training in religious education and were often victimized by their own countrymen.

To the contrary, much like the sub-Saharan Africans cited in the 2017 Migration Policy Institute study, the Angolans of 1619 who were brought to Virginia were better skilled in the trades needed to succeed in the failing colony.[245] They were the descendants of Angolans who benefitted from a developed industrial and agricultural-based economy with over one hundred years of trading with the two world super powers, Spain and Portugal. The *Bautista* Angolans were the beneficiaries of previous generations who learned from the Catholic missionaries and benefited from their own who were sent abroad to Europe to the universities in many of the more developed cities on the Iberian Peninsula and in Rome. They purportedly came from the higher ranks of Angola's tiered society, and it is for that very reason that they were chosen by the Portuguese to be the first ones to be captured, enslaved and sent overseas.

The *Bautista* Angolans became essential to the economic growth of the Virginia colony and to the specific plantations in which they resided. Kidnapped from their native land and brought against their will, the

Angolans brought the necessary skills that the English immigrants lacked, and it is with these skills that the colony survived then eventually prospered. They arrived with distinct skills in agriculture, animal husbandry and the cultivation of tobacco plants and other specialized crops needed for the success of the failed Virginia colony. Not only were the Angolans unique in the skills that they brought to a colony on the brink of collapse, but they also helped to ensure its long-term viability, success and prosperity. Despite the odds, the Angolans succeeded at a time when every conceivable obstacle was placed before them, including nationality, race, language, religion and a well-developed caste system imported from England.

The knowledge, skills and abilities of the Angolans made them unique in many ways. Having descended from their great elders, who had domesticated animals for centuries, they were herders experienced in animal husbandry in ways the English in the colony were not. They were farmers, and they inherently understood agricultural techniques in a subtropical climate, particularly the importance of crop rotation in order to maximize profits.[246] They were taught catechism by the Catholic nuns and missionaries, were able to read and write and had mathematical computation skills necessary to bargain and trade effectively, as evidenced by the early colonial records in Virginia documenting the substantial number of contracts they independently executed. When the Angolans were put to work in the Virginia colony, their value was instantly recognizable; the plantations on which they lived immediately increased crop production and quickly began to turn profits never realized before, also as evidenced by documented records found in the colonial registries. Some historians have postulated that the Angolans' value was so important to the vitality and sustainability of the colony and its newly found cash crop of tobacco that they were immediately enslaved for perpetuity.

The time during which the Angolans arrived and lived most of their lives in the Virginia colony was a period where all men and women, except for the Indigenous Americans, came from some other foreign land. The assumption that their arrival immediately made them enslaved, particularly since they were incredibly valuable and lacked written contracts, oversimplifies the legal condition of all of those who arrived and lived in Virginia during this period of the failed colonial experiment of the Virginia Company. While the *Tarzan* metaphor is an appropriate one, in that it helped to foster certain stereotypical beliefs about Africans, for many, our understanding of antebellum slavery is also embedded in another widely circulated movie,

Gone with the Wind, a fictionalized and romanticized account of the American South prior to the Civil War and the Reconstruction period depicting the "glory" days of slavery.

While the entertainment industry, pop culture and even periods of divisive political rhetoric have done much to shape our opinion and understanding about the continent of Africa, of its people and of American slavery, the period of antebellum slavery is a dark stain on American history, clearly defined by specific, deliberate laws and attitudes that resulted in the horrific treatment of a large segment of the American population who were kidnapped and descended from Africa. Although some may take issue with the argument that white and black indentures had analogous experiences in the early 1600s, compared to their disparate treatment in later years, the documentation clearly supports that English poor were treated similarly to the black indentures, often rather poorly, whether they had indentured contracts or not. While there were substantially more English poor than African poor in Virginia without contracts, no one would ever consider referring to bound Englishmen as inherently enslaved, reflecting a deep-rooted but false belief that skin color was an innate factor in one's legal status; this belief was not introduced until decades later, in response to the Angolans' deft manipulation of the already-existing Virginia Common Laws.

Another premise that the Angolans were enslaved for perpetuity in the Virginia settlement is predicated on a notion that the English settlers, particularly the founding fathers who were sea captains—who sailed the world and visited various ports—were well acquainted with the legal concepts of slavery and servitude and thereby immediately made the Africans enslaved. As cited by historian Norman Davies, slavery in England "remained a well-established trade until the twelfth century," and the "ten percent of England's population during this period who were enslaved were almost entirely of local European origin, most frequently being drawn from prisoners of war," and drawn from internal rebellions.[247] As the Angolans came from a culture that had its own history of enslaving people to slavery, in observing the Spanish and Portuguese who dominated the trade across the sixteenth and early seventeenth centuries, for some historians, the unfounded presumption is that the English would have inherently cast its first Africans to a life of perpetual enslavement once they arrived on the Virginia shores.

However, for historians who hold to these beliefs and have reasoned that the first Africans, and in particular the Angolans from the *San Juan Bautista*, were slaves within the Virginia colony, they find no physical or primary source evidence on which to base this claim, other than they were Africans and that their skin color was black. Again, this default position reflects the later influence of white supremacy on the historical record, rather than a basis of appropriate evidence. It is correct that the Portuguese had captured these Angolan men, women and children, marched them over one hundred miles to the port of Luanda and forced them to board a slave ship under contract to Vera Cruz, New Spain. Their destiny was to be enslaved for perpetuity upon arrival at their designated port. However, while there is no question that the *Bautista* Angolans were captured by the Portuguese to be sold as slaves in the Spanish colony, there is no indication the Virginia colony had a legal system for slavery, so the Angolans were not immediately enslaved; evidence found in the colonial records clearly suggests that enslavement would not be their fate.[248]

Unlike the Spanish and Portuguese, up until the late sixteenth century, English involvement in the transatlantic slave trade was limited. When the two English pirate ships *White Lion* and the *Treasurer* plundered the *San Juan Battista*, they were not looking for enslaved Africans, they were looking to steal Spanish gold and silver. The Angolans on board, much to the dismay of the English pirates, were ill-gotten and unwanted gains and a consolation price that would eventually place the captains and ship owners in tremendous peril legally and politically.

While the documentation on the Angolans is limited but growing, the records of colonial Virginia during this period of history is voluminous, and clear evidence suggests that in 1619, approximately 75 to 80 percent of the English were bonded servants who served their masters in conditions no different from that of the first-generation Angolans. While some may argue that the bonded servitude of the poor and disenfranchised English during this period was no different than the conditions of many of the enslaved Africans and their descendants during antebellum slavery, the parallels nonetheless are remarkably similar on many levels.

When the *San Juan Bautista* Angolans arrived in 1619, there were no laws either found in English Common Law or codified by the newly formed colonial government in Virginia that allowed enslaving people based on race, only contracts that bound the overwhelming majority of the population into indentured servitude. In order to subjugate an entire race of people to generational enslavement, the laws needed to change slowly and methodically by casting as broad a net as possible, ensuring that at the time of birth a child would be bound to perpetuity enslavement.

When a multiracial young woman born to an African servant woman and a white landowner sued for her freedom and her inheritance from her father upon his death, absent a law to the contrary, Elizabeth Key won her 1656 case. However, the gains and accomplishments of the earliest African arrivals in the Virginia colony quickly alerted white colonists to the Angolans' legal savvy and served as the precursor to a series of laws that would dramatically restrict the rights of others and eventually turn them into chattel property.

As in the case of Elizabeth Key, her success was limited and became the foundation for apartheid-type laws when the Virginia Assembly in 1662 later enacted a law that any child born to an enslaved woman would himself or herself become a slave, even if the father were white, reversing hundreds of years of Western Civilization doctrine on inheritance.[249] A half century after the arrival of the first documented Africans, the Key case would become the first legislative act that would eventually lead to a compendium of laws legalizing a sweeping policy of racial segregation and repression and political and economic discrimination in the colony to become known as the Virginia 1705 Slave Codes. The historic and symbolic date of August 25, 1619, was a watershed moment in American history, forcing historians and scholars to rethink the historical importance of the arrival of the first documented Africans in English North America and their direct and indirect impact on the evolution of the slave codes and the national stain of antebellum slavery on American soil.

Despite Americans trying to rationalize and justify race-based American slavery, the capture of the *San Juan Bautista* Angolans does not fit into a neat little box that some would like for us to believe and that most of us were taught. The economies of late sixteenth- and seventeenth-century Portugal and Spain were based on the profits made as a direct result of the African slave trade, and seeing the profits to be made, England followed suit one hundred years later. While historians have in the past postulated that the transatlantic slave trade could not have been possible without African cooperation, the capture of the *Bautista* Angolans was not done at the hands of a competitive warring African nation. Portugal and Spain under the Iberian Union clearly wanted to eradicate the indigenous Angolans from their land to gain access to the valuable silver mines that lay below their feet. The objective of the rulers of the Iberian Union was not to send one ship to buy captured Africans and sell them as slaves; instead, they sent thirty-six ships to conquer a people and their land for the profit and greed.

While the Angolans from the *San Juan Bautista* were not the first Africans in North America, their well-documented transport during the transatlantic slave trade serves as a historic marker going forward to develop a better understanding of the genesis of antebellum slavery, which grew in direct response to the *San Juan Bautista* Angolans.[250] The unique window of opportunity in which the Angolans of the *San Juan Bautista* took full advantage was reversed for other Africans after Bacon's Rebellion, as evidenced by the enactment of the 1705 Slave Codes. It is within the body of these codes that the ugly head of antebellum slavery spawned and spread throughout English North America.

The Angolans who arrived in 1619 managed to live and even prosper during an extraordinarily brief period in American history that was unique from the experiences of the millions of other Africans who followed and endured the indignities and hardships of antebellum slavery. There is no reputable comparison that can be made between the free living conditions of the first-generation Angolans of the *San Juan Bautista* in colonial Virginia and the millions of other Africans who lived as chattel property under the race-based slave laws of Virginia during the century leading up to and the period formally known as the period of antebellum slavery.

In 1607, the shareholders of the Virginia Company of London intended to colonize America and be awarded with handsome profits. They along with the colony's founders intended to use the abundant labor surplus of their country's poor as a cheap inexpensive labor. There does not exist any documentation that the Virginia Company and/or those who came to lead and develop the colony intended to use African labor to meet the colony's workforce needs. The Angolans' arrival on August 25, 1619, was circumstantial but nonetheless consequential and would have a profound impact on the colony's future and its ultimate survival.

While the history of the Angolans of the *San Juan Bautista* may appear to be complete, the details of their saga remain incomplete. Until further research is conducted to shed additional light on who they were and the lives they lived and the legacies they left behind, the full story will continue to be untold. An example of such groundbreaking research was that found by Engel Sluiter and documented in his 1997 article "New Light on the '20 and Odd' Africans Arriving in Virginia."[251]

Without such research, future generations would never have known the rich vibrant city that the *Bautista* Angolans came from and how they arrived with the Spanish/Portuguese names they possessed as found in the colonial Muster of 1624–1625. Sluiter's work also brings to light the role of the

Spanish ambassador Diego Sarmiento de Acuña, the Count of Gondomar. At his insistence, King James's Privy Council investigated the pirating of the *San Juan Bautista,* the slaver of which the count's cousin Manuel Mendes de Acuña was captain. It is from this research that we learn who the *Bautista* Angolans were, the environment and conditions from which they came and how their expertise benefited the failed Jamestown experiment.

The story and the legacy of the Angolans of the *San Juan Bautista* will continue to be researched, as more historians explore and add their own insights into the founders of today's black America. Their story is not one to change a narrative glorifying their fate as that not of an enslaved person, but to shed new light on the history and conditions of the first Africans in what was then called English North America. It's not a story invoking a certain type of status of these Africans or their descendants over the status of any other group of men, women or children from the African continent but sheds light on African life in the colony, even if it was for just a brief moment into American history.

When the charter of the Virginia Company of London was revoked in 1624, the first royal governor, Sir Francis Wyatt, was selected by King James, and he commissioned a new muster under the royal charter in order to determine the colony's population and other sundry details about its inhabitants and property owned.

Between January 20 and February 7, 1625, the survey determined that there were 1,232 inhabitants in the colony, including 23 Angolans. While seldom cited by historians if ever, the muster discloses the first names of a majority of the Angolans and lists the settlement in which they lived in the colony along the James River.

But what is most remarkable is that the English captains—who were purportedly most familiar with the institution of race-based slavery and had been exposed to it in their travels around the world—one by one reported in their musters that the legal status of the Angolans from the *San Juan Bautista* was that of servants and not that of slaves, as found in the primary-source documents in the colonial records.[252]

The cancerous growth of antebellum slavery was fueled by the transatlantic slave trade, the largest forced migration of people. Over 12 million men, women and children were taken from Africa and transported to other continents. While only 10 million Africans arrived at their final port of call, they each brought to the New World different skills and abilities that benefited the countries in which they landed. It is from these Africans and their descendants that world economies were built and Western Civilization prospered and advanced. We know today that of the 10 million who survived the Middle Passage, only 350,326 Africans were brought to the United States, then known as English North America, who became the ancestors of many of today's Americans of African descent.[253]

The transatlantic slave trade was not just about the number of men, women and children who were kidnapped from Africa and sold worldwide; it's a story of honored ancestors who survived a horrific journey in the belly of slavers' cargo holds, of their personal perseverance after being ripped from their families and of their survival under the most inhumane living and working conditions known to mankind.

CHRONOLOGY

AD 1180	Kindom of Kongo is founded.
1442	First West African enslaved are taken to Lisbon, Spain.
1483	Portuguese navigator Diogo Cão discovers Kongo Kingdom; Portugal establishes relations with Angola.
1485	King Njinga Nkuwu of Kongo is baptized and rules as King João I.
1492	Christopher Columbus attempts to sails to India.
1506	King Njinga Nkuwu dies, son Njinga Mbemba rules as King Afonso.
1513	King Afonso I attacks rebel Ndongo Kingdom.
1518	Ndongo Kingdom requests independence from Kongo.
1520	King Afonso I of Kongo establishes Christianity as national religion; Portuguese missionaries sent to Ndongo to set up independence mission are unsuccessful.
1526	King Afonso I sends letter to Portugal's king complaining about African slave trade.
1543	King Afonso I dies.
1545	King Diogo I is crowned as new king of Kondo Kingdom.
1550	Independent Ndongo Kingdom is founded.

1560	A second Portuguese mission, led by Paulo Dias de Novais, is sent to Ndongo.
1564	Portuguese explorer Dias de Novais secures a grant allowing him to colonize Angola (Ndongo).
1575	Portuguese under Dias de Novais found São Paulo de Loanda, capital of Angola; the Portuguese colony of Angola is founded.
1580	The Kingdoms of Portugal and Spain are united, with the union lasting until 1640.
1589	Paulo Dias de Novais, supported by King Álvaro I of Kongo, sends a large army to attack Angola. Portuguese/Kongoese army is defeated at the Battle of Lukala.
1595	The Pope declares Portuguese colony of Kongo to be an "episcopal see," the seat of the Catholic bishop, with jurisdiction over both Kongo and Angola
1599	Portugal and Ndongo sign a peace treaty and formalize relationships.
1606	April 10: England's King James I grants the Virginia Company Charter to establish a settlement in the Chesapeake region of North America.
1607	May 4: Captain Christopher Newport's three ships land on the Jamestown peninsula to establish an English colony.
	May 14: English land 105 men to begin building Jamestown.
	December 29: Captain John Smith first meets Chief Powhattan.
1608	January 7: Jamestown colony is almost destroyed by fire.
1609	May 23: Virginia Company of London Second Charter, responsible for colony administration, allows for selling shares to raise needed funds for expansion.
	October 1: First English women arrive in Jamestown
1609/10	The winter of the starving time.
1611	John Rolfe imports tobacco seeds.
1613	April 13: Pocahontas is captured and brought to Jamestown.
1614	John Rolfe makes first shipment of Virginia West Indian tobacco to England.

1616	John Rolfe, Pocahontas and their son go to England on board the *Treasurer*; the concept of one hundred acres or "hundreds" begin, eventually to be known as "plantations."
1617	March 21: Pocahontas dies in England.
	Captain Samuel Argall becomes new deputy governor, replacing George Yeardley.
1618	Governor Luís Mendes de Vasconcellos wages successful war on Ndongo against the Kimbundu-speaking people, capturing thousands; Chief Powhatan dies, younger half-brother Opechancanough takes charge of federation.
1619	January: George Yeardley returns as governor of Virginia, given special orders by the Virginia Company.
	Early Spring: Slave ship *San Juan Bautista* leaves the port of São Paulo de Loanda and sets sail from Angola to Vera Cruz, New Spain (Mexico).
	July 30: Governor Yeardley convenes the Virginia General Assembly of the colony of Virginia, the first representative assembly in English America.
	July–August: *San Juan Bautista* is pirated; human cargo arrives in Jamestown, Virginia.
	August 25: First Africans arrive in Virginia. Governor Yeardley and his cape merchant place fourteen Africans on their plantations.
	August 30: Captain de Acuña of the Portuguese slave ship *San Juan Bautista* arrives in Vera Cruz, New Spain, with a cargo of only 147 slaves.
1620	March: Virginia's first muster, or census, is compiled and lists 892 Europeans and, among "Others not Christians in the Service of the English," 4 Indians and 32 Africans (15 male, 17 female).
	December: Plymouth Colony is founded in what was initially referred to as "northeast Virginia."
1621	An African named Antonio arrives in Virginia aboard the *James*. The following March, he will be one of only a handful of people who manage to survive an Indian attack on the plantation of Edward Bennett.

1622	An African woman named Mary arrives in Virginia aboard the *Margaret and John*.
	Opechancanough leads the Powhatan Nation in an uprising; approximately one third of the 1,200 colonists in Virginia are massacred, to be known at the Powhatan's Massacre of 1622. Starts long ten-year war between the English and the Powhatans.
1623	King James's Privy Council investigates conditions in Virginia and the Virginia Company of Virginia.
1624	February: The population of Europeans in the Virginia colony is 906. A muster, or census, lists 21 Africans, down from 32 in 1620; 12 of the Africans are identified by name, suggesting they have been baptized.
	Virginia Company of Virginia loses its charter, Virginia becomes a royal colony.
1625	January 20–February 7: The population of Europeans in the Virginia colony is 1,232. The muster lists 23 Africans and 1 Indigenous American, all of them with the legal designation of servants. They live on plantations scattered from the mouth of the James River to Flowerdew Hundred.
1627	Tobacco exports soar to about 500,000 pounds in this year, requiring additional labor.
1628	The African population in Virginia rises dramatically when the ship *Fortune*, out of Massachusetts Bay, captures a Portuguese slaver carrying about one hundred Angolans, whom the captain sells in Virginia for tobacco.
1629	Massachusetts, by statute, becomes the first slaveholding colony in English North America.
1630	Large numbers of European male indentured servants begin to arrive in Virginia to work tobacco fields.
	Virginia General Assembly passes law to restrict personal relationships between Africans and Europeans.
1634	Virginia is divided into eight shires with the colonial office of sheriff as the chief administrator.
	Across the Chesapeake Bay, Lord Baltimore establishes the colony of Maryland, which attracts English Catholics.

1639/49	Virginia General Assembly passes law excluding blacks from the requirement of possessing arms.
1641	Sir William Berkeley, appointed governor of Virginia, arrives in the colony the following year.
1642	Virginia General Assembly passes fugitive Slave Order.
1642	Virginia General Assembly defines black women as tithables (taxable), creating a distinction between African and English women.
1645	English North America enters slave trade directly with Africa, when Boston ship *Rainbow* sails to Africa.
1645	All black men and women, and all other men between the ages of sixteen to sixty, to be considered tithes.
1646	Opechancanough is finally captured and killed at Jamestown. A treaty of peace ends the Anglo-Powhatan War.

GLOSSARY

ANGOLA. The name *Angola* first appears in the Dias de Novais's royal charter in 1571. It covers the land mass in central West Africa between the Kwanza and Lukala Rivers. The area was nominally a possession of the Kingdom of Kongo but became independent in the sixteenth century.

ANTEBELLUM. The period between 1820 and 1865, at the height and perhaps during the "darkest hours" of American slavery until the end of the Civil War. The genesis of the antebellum period commenced with the enactment of the Slave Codes in 1705 in the colony of Virginia and spread throughout the South when other colonies, then states subsequently passed similar laws restricting the rights of Africans and African descendants.

CAPE MERCHANT. The Virginia colony supply officer and trade agent responsible for food and supplies.

CENSUS. A record all the inhabitants of the colony at the time, it captures demographic information such as names, place of residence and ship of arrival.

CHARTER GENERATION. Used to describe the first- and second-generation Angolans brought to English North America who for the most part operated outside of and within the indentured system initially and eventually the slave system of colonial Virginia. They married and intermarried with one another as well with the native indigenous people and the English.

CORSAIR. A pirate ship hired or authorized to conduct raids on ships of an enemy country and split proceeds between the entity who contracted the privateers and the privateers.

EMANCIPATION. The liberation or the act of being set free from restraint or domination.

ENCUMBERED. During the period when the Virginia Company of London managed the colony, with the exception of the shareholders, all residents were restricted in such a way that they were not free in their actions.

ENSLAVED. A person subjugated to another person without having any independent rights or privileges.

FOLIO. A method of page numbering in a book, occurring on the front side of the page.

FREEMAN. A person who either inherits or is given full liberties and is not encumbered by any legal restriction.

FREE PEOPLE OF COLOR. Men, women or children who are of African or mixed-race descent who lived in colonial or antebellum America and were born free, became free or escaped to freedom before the institution of enslavement was abolished in 1865.

GALLEON. Fifteenth- and sixteenth-century multi-masted ship built for war and large enough to carry cargo on its multitiered decks.

HEADRIGHT. The allotment of fifty acres of land to someone who paid the transportation costs for himself or another to come to Virginia.

INDENTURE. A legally binding document for contract labor with established time duration.

INDENTURED SERVANT. A person who agreed to enter into an indenture contract for a set period of time and without pay in exchange for passage to America.

KIMBUNDU. Language of the Mbundu people from central West Africa.

KONGO. One of the great Bakongo nations in central West Africa.

LEASEHOLD. The ownership of a temporary right to hold land or property in which a lessee or a tenant holds rights of real property by some form of title from a lessor or landlord.

LETTER OF MARQUE. A government-approved license to authorize a person, known as a privateer or corsair, to attack and capture enemy vessels and to commit acts that would otherwise have constituted piracy.

LIMBO. An intermediate or transitional state in which a person or group of people has no legal status.

MASTER. One who owns the contract of an indentured servant, or who owns and controls the life and action(s) of another person.

MBUNDU. The nation of Kimbundu-speaking people in central West Africa, composed of a number of kingdoms or states.

MERCENARY. An individual or group of individuals hired to take part in an armed conflict who is not part of a regular army or government.

MUSTER. Includes information on the inhabitants of the colony and data on livestock, buildings or land.

NDONGO. An early modern African state first recorded in the sixteenth century. It was one of a number of vassal states to Kongo, though Ndongo was the most powerful of these, with a king called the Ngola.

NGOLA. Kimbundu term used for the title of king of Ndongo.

PAPAL BULL. A written proclamation, letter, charter or public decree issued by the pope of the Catholic Church.

PIRACY. The act of robbery or criminal violence by ship or boat on the high seas.

PREPONDERANCE OF EVIDENCE. In law, history and genealogy, the clear and convincing evidence, beyond reasonable doubt and its probable truth or accuracy is true, and not on the amount of evidence.

SLAVE. A person and their descendants who are the legal property of another for perpetuity and are forced by law to be under their control.

SLAVE SHIPS. See the definition for a galleon ship.

TITHABLES. A person who is capable of working in the labor force and is responsible to pay a tax to contribute to the welfare of the local community.

TITHE. A portion of one's annual tobacco production or earnings, taken as a tax for the support of the church or county administration.

TREASON. Betraying one's country or attempting to overthrow one's government.

NOTES

Preface

1. According to the creators, David Eltis and Paul F. Lachance, the Trans-Atlantic Slave Trade Database comprises more than thirty-five thousand individual slaving expeditions between 1514 and 1866. Records of the voyages have been found in archives and libraries throughout the Atlantic world. They provide information about vessels, enslaved peoples, slave traders and owners and trading routes. The database cites the records for each voyage in the database. Other variables enable users to search for information about a particular voyage or group of voyages. The interactive website provides full capability to analyze the data and report results in the form of statistical tables, graphs, maps, a timeline and an animation.

2. A clear distinction must be made between the first documented Africans in North America and the first documented Africans in English North America (the United States). In 1526, Africans were documented as part of a Spanish expedition to present-day South Carolina, and in 1565, the Spanish once again brought Africans to St. Augustine in present-day Florida. U.S. history is based on English North America going forward, and thus the distinction of the first documented Africans in English North America. Archaeological discoveries have found remains of Africans in parts of present-day Central and South America predating those mentioned.

3. During the period in which the "20 and Odd" arrived in English North America, the Spanish and the Portuguese referred to Africans as men and women who were black, hence the Spanish word *negro* was used to describe skin color. The word did not translate to English, and instead of describing the Africans as having black skin, the English began to use the word *negro* as a noun.

4. William Waller Hening (1768–1828), nineteenth-century attorney and publisher, best known for his codification of the Commonwealth of Virginia's laws from 1619 to 1792, along with an extensive appendix.

Introduction

5. As described in more detail later, the actual term used by John Rolfe was the "20 and Odd Negroes." Rolfe intended to mislead representatives of the Virginia Company in London and King James's Privy Council; the actual number of Angolans that arrived in the Virginia colony was much greater. Therefore, the phrase is specious at best. For the past four hundred years, historians have continued to use this verbiage to describe the men, women and children who were pirated from the *San Juan Bautista*. However, more appropriate language would refer to them as the Angolans from the *San Juan Bautista*, and in this text, out of respect for who they were and all that they accomplished under unusual circumstances, that (and other variations) is how they will be referred to.

6. Emory University, "Voyages: The Trans-Atlantic Slave Trade Database," http://slavevoyages.org [hereafter Voyages database].

7. In 1607, Captain John Smith named the land along the body of water known as Hampton Roads as Point Comfort. The land was renamed in the 1630s as Old Point Comfort after the development of an area named New Point Comfort.

8. Dawsey, "Trump Derides Protections for Immigrants from 'Shithole' Counties."

9. Simmons, "African Immigrants Are More Educated than Most."

10. Echeverria-Estrada and Batalova, "Sub-Saharan African Immigrants in the United States," Migration Policy Instute, www.migrationpolicy. org. The research was compiled from the following sources: Migration Policy Institute; Department of Homeland Security (DHS), Office of Immigration Statistics; U.S. Census Bureau; University of Minnesota; and the World Bank Prospects Group.

Chapter 1

11. An appointed individual who in the colony served as a government official with the power to receive, promote, defend, audit or determine an opinion on behalf of the colony.
12. De Villiers and Hirtle, *Into Africa*, 158.
13. Hashaw, *Birth of Black America*, 15.
14. Thomas, *Story of the Atlantic Slave Trade*, 82.
15. According to John Thornton, professor of African American Studies and History, Boston University, the proper ethnonym that should be applied to the people of Kongo is Kongolese, and that usage will be used throughout.
16. Thomas, *Story of the Atlantic Slave Trade*, 82.
17. De Villiers and Hirtle, *Into Africa*, 161.
18. Shillington, *History of Africa*, 201.
19. According to John Thornton, professor of African American Studies and History, Boston University, the proper ethnonym that should be applied to the people of Ndongo is Ndongos, and that usage will be used throughout.
20. Thornton, "African Experience," 428.
21. Sluiter, "New Light on the '20 and Odd' Africans Arriving in Virginia in 1619," 397.
22. Thornton, "African Experience," 424, 431–34. See also Heintze, *Das Ende*, 115.
23. Sluiter, "New Light," 396–97.
24. We know the actual number of Africans aboard the slaver *San Juan Bautista* based on the contract the ship's captain, Manuel Mendes de Acuña, had with Antonio Fernandes Delvas in Angola, where Acuña was to deliver his shipment of 350 Africans to Vera Cruz, New Spain. See also Sluiter, "New Light," 397.
25. Sluiter, "New Light," 397.
26. Hashaw, *Birth of Black America*, 69.
27. Ibid.
28. Brown, *Genesis of the United States*, 885.
29. Hashaw, *Birth of Black America*, 73.
30. Kingsbury, *Records of the Virginia*, 3:243. The specific letter is identified as *John Rolfe, A Letter to Sir Edwin Sandys, January 1619/20* [hereafter Rolfe to Sandys 1619/20], Ferrar Papers [hereafter FP], Autograph Letter, Signed, with Seals List of Records No. 154.

31. Sluiter, "New Light," 397. The *San Juan Bautista* was so badly damaged during battle with the *Treasurer* and the *White Lion* that the Angolans were eventually transferred to the *Santa Ana*, and it was that vessel that brought them to shore at Vera Cruz.

32. According to the Muster of 1625, Angelo was listed on the Muster, and according to said document she arrived on board the *Treasurer*. Since there is no credible evidence that once the *Treasurer* left Point Comfort for Bermuda it ever returned, the preponderance of evidence would clearly suggest that she departed at this point in time. Over time, her name was changed to read Angela in the colonial records. See Hotten, *Original Lists of Persons of Quality*, 174, 224.

33. Sluiter, "New Light," 398.

34. Voyages database.

35. King James was the son of Mary, Queen of Scotland, and her second husband, Henry Stuart, Lord Darnley, thus starting the Stuart dynasty. Born a Catholic, Mary was the only surviving legitimate child of King James V and perceived by many to be the legitimate heir to the English monarchy. Her cousin Queen Elizabeth, a Protestant, was the reigning monarch of England was considered by many as not the rightful heir to the English throne. However, since England was a devout Protestant nation, Mary was never installed as the rightful heir to the English throne. When Elizabeth died childless, the English monarchy reverted to James, the son of her Catholic cousin, Mary, Queen of Scotland.

36. Kingsbury, *Records of the Virginia Company*, 3:241–43.

37. Ibid.

38. Thornton, "African Experience," 103.

39. Kingsbury, *Records of the Virginia Company*, 3:241–43, Rolfe to Sandys 1619/20, FP.

40. An officer of the ship and an Angolan woman were sent ashore and left behind; see preface.

41. Hashaw, Hashaw, *Birth of Black America*, 109.

42. Craven, *Dissolution of the Virginia Company*, 177.

43. Ibid., 39.

44. In the book *English Adventurers and Emigrants*, noted historian Peter Wilson Coldham mistakenly transcribed the testimony of deponent John Wood in the case *Robert, Earl of Warwick v. Edward Brewster*. Coldham wrote the despondent testified that "after the *Treasurer* returned from Bermuda to Virginia she was taken into a creek where she overturned and was sunk. Her company went ashore to live." However, the transcription was in

error and was corrected by the expert research of noted Virginia colony historian and author Martha McCartney. She found that Wood's correct testimony on the *Treasurer* is that it "went from Virginia to the Somer Islands where there was also a scarcity of victuals and thence set out for the West Indies to seek victuals and that place would not then supply the *Treasurer* there, Mr. and captain of her being they could not carry out her forward course for want of victuals, by the governors consent he took her Ordnance, carried her into a creek and here would her lie and the men forsake her and went ashore here and lived and when a while after the ship the *Treasurer* overset and sunk in the water past all recovery." The *Treasurer* never left Bermuda and was sunk there and not in Virginia. See Coldham, *English Adventurers and Emigrants*, 13. McCartney's assessment would be confirmed by a letter from Governor Nathaniel Butler to the company's engineer requesting that the *Treasurer* be taken apart. See also Lefroy, *Memorials of the Discovery*, 252.

45. When the *White Lion* arrived in the colony, Governor Yeardley and cape merchant Piersey, two men not favorable to the Earl of Warwick, took all of the available Angolans to their respective plantations. On the subsequent arrival of additional Angolans, originally from the *Treasurer*'s portion in Bermuda, they were dispersed to the plantations of men who were favorable to the interests of Warwick.

46. Bridenbaugh, *Jamestown*, 29.

47. FP, vol. 33, no. 3, Summer 1995, 168. The census and other legal documents usually start with a March date. Until 1752, England and its colonies followed the Julian calendar, with March 25 being the first day of the calendar year (in other words, comparable to present-day January being the first day of the new year). Within a number of colonial records, legal documents will have two calendar year dates on the document. Therefore there may be slight variances between calendar years depending on whether a Julian or Gregorian calendar was used in the source documentation. During the transition period between the two calendars, dual dating was used, as found in many early colonial Virginia documents.

48. Hashaw, *Birth of Black America*, 159.

Chapter 2

49. Tolan, Veinstein and Laurens, *Europe and the Islamic World*, 164. The term *Saracen* in European languages was meant to mean being a "Turk" or of

being of the Muslim faith. "To become a Turk," for example, became the ordinary expression for the act of converting to Islam.

50. Unam Sanctum Catholicam, "Dum Diversas (English Translation)."

51. Pope Nicolas V, *Romanus Pontifex*, January 8, 1455. See Hock, *When Ancestors Weep*, Appendix A, "The Doctrine of Discovery."

52. Phillips, *Holy Warriors*, 305.

53. Ibid.

54. Hashaw, *Birth of Black America*, 15.

55. De Villiers and Hirtle, *Into Africa*, 158.

56. Wallenfeldt, *Africa to America*, 65.

57. Niane, *Africa from the Twelfth to the Sixteenth Century*, 574.

58. Ibid., 574–75.

59. Ibid., 576.

60. Thomas, *Story of the Atlantic Slave Trade*, 81.

61. Ibid., 81–82.

62. Van Reybrouck, *Congo*, 21.

63. Thomas, *Story of the Atlantic Slave Trade*, 82.

64. Ibid.

65. De Villiers and Hirtle, *Into Africa*, 161.

66. Hashaw, *Birth of Black America*, 29–30.

67. Van Reybrouck, *Congo*, 22.

68. De Villiers and Hirtle, *Into Africa*, 161.

69. Ibid., 162.

70. Battell, *Strange Adventures*, 117.

71. De Villiers and Hirtle, *Into Africa*, 165.

72. Ibid.

73. Appiah and Gates, *Africana*, 4:190.

74. De Villiers and Hirtle, *Into Africa*, 166–67.

75. Ibid.

76. Paulo Dias de Novais was the grandson of Portuguese Bartolomeu Dias, an explorer known as the first to sail around the Horn of Africa in 1488, thereby setting up a trade route between Europe and Asia.

77. De Villiers and Hirtle, *Into Africa*, 167.

78. Shillington, *History of Africa*, 201.

79. Ibid.

80. Battell, *Strange Adventures*, 144.

81. Ibid., 147.

82. Ibid., 147n3.

83. Ibid., 149.

Chapter 3

84. Kingsbury, *Records of the Virginia Company*, 3:543. "A Declaration of the State of the Colony and Affairs of Virginia…and a Relation of the Barbarous Massacre."

85. McMillan, *Sir Walter Raleigh's Lost Colony*, 5.

86. Ibid.

87. Hening, *Statues at Large*, 1:57–66.

88. Ibid.

89. McMillan, *Sir Walter Raleigh's Lost Colony*, 5.

90. Glover and Smith, *Shipwreck that Saved Jamestown*, 34.

91. Williams, *Jamestown Experiment*, 55.

92. Arber, *Travels and Works of Captain John Smith*, xliv.

93. Ibid., l–li.

94. Ibid., 6–7.

95. Ibid., lxx.

96. Glover and Smith, *Shipwreck that Saved Jamestown*, 42.

97. McCary, *Indians in Seventeenth-Century Virginia*, 1.

98. Axtell, *Rise and Fall of the Powhatan Empire*, 5.

99. Ibid, 7.

100. Hatch, *First Seventeen Years*, 6.

101. Neill, *History of the Virginia Company*, 23.

102. Bemiss, *Three Charters*, 17.

103. Robinson, *Mother Earth*, 14.

104. Williams, *Jamestown Experiment*, 134.

105. Hatch, *First Seventeen Years*, 8.

106. Ibid., 10.

107. Bridenbaugh, *Jamestown*, 45.

108. Williams, *Jamestown Experiment*, 193–94. See also Haile, *Jamestown Narratives*, 419, 505, 913.

109. Hatch, *First Seventeen Years*, 12–13.

110. Bridenbaugh, *Jamestown*, 41.

111. Although Rebecca Rolfe's death throughout history has been reported to have been from tuberculosis, many believed then that her death was not from natural causes and that her husband's association with some of the wealthy in England may have been behind her death.

112. Bridenbaugh, *Jamestown*, 39–40.

113. Kingsbury, *Records of the Virginia Company*, 3:70–72, Rolfe to Sandys 1619/20, FP.

114. Williams, *Jamestown Experiment*, 237.
115. Marshal, *Jamestown Century*, 24.
116. Woolley, *Savage Kingdom*, 18.
117. Bruce, *Virginia*, 108. Bruce was an attorney in the state of Virginia and served as the centennial historian of the University of Virginia and the corresponding secretary of the Virginia Historical Society.
118. Ibid.
119. Ibid., 108–10.
120. Ibid., 110.
121. Jester and Woodroof, *Adventurers of Purse and Person*, 10.
122. Craven, *Virginia Company of London*, 180–83.

Chapter 4

123. De Villiers and Hirtle, *Into Africa*, 166–67.
124. Thornton, "African Experience," 432 n40; Francisco de Gouvela to Jesuit general, November 1, 1564, in Brasio, *Monumenta Missionaria Africana*, 15:230–31. This is the original version of a text printed from a copy. Although the text is from more than fifty years before, it is the only description of the capital of Ndongo. For a description of Kongo's capital and central African cities in general see Thornton, "Mbanza Kongo/Sao Salvador" in Anderson and Rachbone, *Africa's Urban Past*, 67–79.
125. Appiah and Gates, *Africana*, 4:191
126. Cadornega, *Historia Geral*, 1:83. These notes were collected from recollections of contemporaries by the soldier-chronicler who arrived in Angola in 1639 and wrote his account in 1680–81. Although based on original materials, early portions of Cardornega's chronicle are sometimes garbled and contain errors of chronology. The treatise by Mendes de Vasconcellos, no longer extant, is circled in Cadornega.
127. The best account of the battle is in Rodrigues, "Historia da Resdencia," 4:574–76.
128. Vasconcellos, "Adbierre de las Cosas," 4:574–76.
129. Montecuccolo, "Missions Evangelica," 11–15. For the interpretation of these highly politicized and manipulated sources see Thornton, "Legitimacy and Political Power," 17–40.
130. Thornton, "African Experience," 424, 431–34. The presidio was moved sometime before 1618, when Baltasar Rebelo de Argao, one of the original conquerors of Angola, wrote his memoirs (a date established

by Brasio as being twenty-five years after his arrival in 1593); Rebelo de Argao to king of Portugal (?) 1618, in Brasio, *Monumenta Missionaria Africana*, 6:334 (date on 343).

131. Thornton, "African Experience," 426. See also Battell, *Strange Adventures*, 21, 31–33. In 1589, twenty-four-year-old Andrew Battell from Essex, England, sailed to the Portuguese colony of Brazil, where he and other crew members became separated. Captured by local Native American tribesmen, Battel and five companions were taken to local Portuguese missionaries. After a four-month imprisonment, he and another Englishman were shipped to the Portuguese island of Luanda off the coast of Africa. After being imprisoned for another four months, he was sent 130 miles up the Kwanza River to another Portuguese outpost. His eighteen years as captive in Africa was chronicled in *The Strange Adventures of Andrew Battel of Leigh*. Battell left the River Thames in England, arrived on the River Plate (Buenos Aires) and was shipped as a Portuguese prisoner to Cape Palmas off the coast of Liberia and Angola. Although some dates and names of certain individuals seem to be inconsistent with current documentation, Battell's firsthand account is deemed highly credible and accurate.

132. The most systematic later account is that of Montecucculo, "Missions Evangelica."

133. Thornton, "African Experience," 428.

134. Ibid., 429.

135. Ibid., 430n31. Faria, "Historia Portugueza," MS 241, fol 163V under date March 1, 1619, to end of February 1620 but related to material of a year earlier (1618–1619); quoted in Cadornega, *Historia Geral*, 1:88–90 n.i. The formation of the Imbangala alliance and movement of the presida is given as 1618 in Manuel Vogado Sotomaior, "Papel Sobre as Cousas de Angola" (undated but probably around 1620) in Brasio, *Monumenta Missionaria Africana*, 15:476 (date on 480).

136. Thornton, "African Experience," 429n28; Soares, "Copia Dos Excessos," 6:368.

137. Thornton, "African Experience," 430. See also 429n28. Soares, Soares, "Copia Dos Excessos," 6:369–70. Vagado Sotomaior, then holding the position of ouvidor geral de Angola, noted that the city of Angola (Kabasa) was "sacked in such a way that many thousands souls were captured, eaten and killed…and all the palm trees were cut down (in Imbangala fashion) so that the area was effectively barren of them."

138. Thornton, "African Experience," 428.

139. Ibid., 424, 431–34n39. See also Heintze, *Das Ende*, 115.
140. Sluiter, "New Light," 396–97.
141. Ibid., 397.

Chapter 5

142. Kingsbury, *Records of the Virginia Company*, 1:107 n(a). The Virginia Company had a large number of records that are no longer extant but have been revealed by a study of the existing documents. In addition to the original court books and the five other records provided by the "Orders and Constitutions," there were the books created at a later date, the duplicates of patents and grants, the petitions and all of the account books of the various magazines and joint stock companies.

143. Introduction to the Records of the Virginia Company of London, Fate of the Original Records. See Kingsbury, *Records of the Virginia Company*, 1:107–8.

144. Craven, *Dissolution of the Virginia Company*, 126.

145. Robert Rich, Second Earl of Warwick (1587–1658), was one of the wealthiest men in England, a major investor in the Virginia Company of London and a prominent Puritan. His religious beliefs and business interests, including his vast shipping empire, often brought him into direct conflicts with the Catholic Spanish monarchy. It was his ship, the *Treasurer*, that created a major international dispute between England and Spain when it attacked in consort the Spanish slaver *San Juan Bautista* and then brought Spanish subjects from Angola to the Virginia and Bermuda colonies. His spacious manor in England, Leighs Priory in Felsted, Essex, was used as a hideout for four of the Angolans. They were concealed from interrogators from the Privy Council interested in determining Warwick's connection to their kidnapping. His business interests included but were not limited to the patent for the Massachusetts Bay Colony; the "Saybrook" patent in Connecticut; and the Somers Isles Company and Providence Island Company. Later in life, he was a strong opponent of King Charles and supported the interests of Lord Cromwell during the English Civil War.

146. Bermuda, originally named the Somers Islands, after English Admiral George Somers. In 1609, en route to Virginia on board the ship *Sea Venture*, Somers got caught in a major storm and became stranded on the island.

147. In a 1621 lawsuit between Earl of Warwick and Edward Bruster "Concerning the Ships 'Treasurer' and 'Neptune,'" it was recorded that the *Treasurer*, when leaving the docks of London, pretended to have fishing equipment, including "salt hooks and lines, fishermen or men skilled in fishing." When it rendezvoused at sea with the *Neptune*, *Treasurer* was equipped with "powder, shot, waistcloths, ordinances, streamers, flags fit for a man-o-war." See PRO List of Records 226. See also Kingsbury, *Records of the Virginia Company*, 3:418.

148. Trevelyan, *Sir Walter Raleigh*, 480–81, 510–16.

149. Rouse, *Sir Walter Raleigh*, 315–18.

150. Craven, *Dissolution of the Virginia Company*, 126–27.

151. Ibid., 127–28.

152. Kingsbury, *Records of the Virginia Company*, 3:119–22.

153. Instructions to Governor Yeardley, 1618, *VMHB*, vol. 2, 1895, 154–55. It should be noted that it has been recorded that numerous Indigenous American nations and tribes had different forms of representative governments; therefore, the author arbitrarily inserted the word *English* to accurately portray the reality of the quote without changing its original intent.

154. Craven, *Dissolution of the Virginia Company*, 46.

155. Ibid. See also Kingsbury, *Records of the Virginia Company*, 2:403–5.

156. Kingsbury, *Records of the Virginia Company*, 3: documents I, 1607–1622, 118–122.

157. Craven, *Dissolution of the Virginia Company*, 130.

158. The Spanish slaver the *San Juan Bautista* was built in Japan in 1613 in preparation of diplomatic relations with the West. Despite best efforts, the diplomatic relations failed, and the ship was eventually sold to Spain, as it was building its naval defenses against the Dutch. See also Boxer, *Christian Century in Japan*.

159. Tyler, *Narratives of Early Virginia*, 282n1.

160. Thornton, "African Experience," 103.

161. Report of the Royal Commission on Historic Manuscripts Public Records Office, Kew, England, courtesy of the LoV, Virginia Colonial Records Project; document no. 261, courtesy of the LoV, Virginia Colonial Records Project, John Dutton to the Earl of Warwick, January 20, 1620. When the *Treasurer* arrived in Bermuda, it had twenty-nine Angolans on board, indicating that one went ashore.

162. Kingsbury, *Records of the Virginia Company*, 3: documents I, 219–20.

163. Tyler, *Narratives of Early Virginia*, 282n1.

164. Hashaw, *Birth of Black America*, 128.

165. Some historians have theorized that the arrival of a shipment of fourteen Africans in Bermuda from a "Dutch frigot" in the fall of 1619 must have come from the *White Lion* since it was flying a Dutch marque. The charade of the *Treasurer*'s Captain Elfrith, the Earl of Warwick and Bermuda's Governor Butler relative to the acts of piracy of the *San Juan Bautista*, coupled with the arrival and placement of the fourteen Africasns in question has aided in this confusion. Sometime before the arrival of the *Treasurer* in Bermuda in the fall of 1619, a Captain Kerby, a known local pirate, entered the port with fourteen Africans from a Dutch slaver. According to Kerby, who was sailing a small barge in the West Indies, a "Dutch frigate...on the western shore" provided him with the fourteen Angolans. Although the arrival of this group of Africans occurred months before the September 1619 arrival of the *Treasurer*, no evidence exists that the Africans were part of the group of Angolans who were originally on board the *San Juan Bautista*. Some historians presumed because of the furor caused by the acts of piracy of the *San Juan Bautista* that the *White Lion* was deemed to have shipwrecked in order to avoid any further questions and that it was the *White Lion* that provided Captain Kerby with fourteen Africans. However, absent primary source evidence, the *White Lion* at no point in this journey was stranded and should not be confused with the Dutch ship that arrived of the coast of Bermuda in February 1620 with Captain Scoutans at the helm, which "cast away upon the Western Shore... yet [aided] by the help of the English they saved the men, though the ship perished amongst the rocks." The English *White Lion*, flying a Dutch marque when it arrived in Virginia, sailed successfully back to England to deliver letters to London from the Virginia colony. Other historians have also postulated that the *White Lion* may have rendezvoused with Captain Kerby prior to his arrival in Bermuda and then transferred fourteen of the *San Juan Bautista* Angolans to him; this theory also is not supported by primary source evidence. See Lefroy, *Memorials of the Discovery*, 147, 150, and 722. See also Wesley Frank Craven, "An Introduction to the History of Bermuda VI, The Revised Plan of Settlement," *W&MQ* 18, no. 1 (1938): 50.

166. In a reflection of the activities surrounding the attack of the *White Lion* and the *Treasurer* against the Spanish slaver the *San Juan Bautista*, in a report it was stated that "It haith been said by many, and particularly by some principal persons of the opposite party, that the dissolutions of these plantations was part of the Count Gondomars Instructions: And certainly

we found his activities in negotiating here instruments of ourselves against ourselves," as found in the Virginia Company, Discourse of the Old Company, April, 1625. C.o. 1, vol. 3, no. 40, document in Public Records Office, Kew, England, List of Records No. 785. See Kingsbury, *Records of the Virginia Company*, 3:539.

167. Kingsbury, *Records of the Virginia Company*, 3:243.

168. The documents and subject matter contained in Kingsbury's *Records of the Virginia Company [of London]* are as stated, "original papers, official and other, of the company or relating to it; and explains the difficulties met and overcome…and record the controversy between the company and the Crown that resulted in the dissolution of the corporation and the creation of the first crown colony of Great Britain."

169. Kingsbury, *Records of the Virginia Company*, 3:243, Rolfe to Sandys 1619/20, FP.

170. The reference to Algiers refers to the area of Northern Africa along the Barbary Coast where some of the fiercest battles took place between warring nations and their corsair agents, who stole from one another with tremendous frequency. See Kingsbury, *Records of the Virginia Company*, 3:367. See also Craven, *Dissolution of the Virginia Company*, 137.

171. Coldham, *English Adventurers and Emigrants*, 13.

172. At least three of the original Angolans from the *San Juan Bautista* would return to Virginia from England on the *James* in 1621, the *Margaret & the Mary* in 1622 and the *Swan* in 1623.

173. Report of the Royal Commission on Historic Manuscripts Public Records Office, Kew, England, courtesy of the LoV, Virginia Colonial Records Project, document no. 275, 35b, Captain Nathaniel Butler, Letter to the Earl of Warwick, October 9, 1620.

174. Coldham, *English Adventurers and Emigrants*, 181. Although Stafford confirms that the Angolans were taken to Bermuda on the *Treasurer*, his number of twenty-five is short of four as documented in previous evidence that the actual number was twenty-nine. In his testimony, he stated that "the *Treasurer* left the Somer Islands in February 1620." This misstatement encouraged historians to believe that *Treasurer* returned to Virginia. However, this has now been refuted by the letter written by Governor Butler to the company's engineer to disassemble the ship in Bermuda in 1622. See Lefroy, *Memorials of the Discovery*, 252.

175. Coldham, *English Adventurers and Emigrants*, 181–82.

176. Ibid., 182.

177. Brown, *First Republic in America*, 359.

178. Report of the Royal Commission on Historic Manuscripts Public Records Office, Kew, England, courtesy of the LoV, Virginia Colonial Records Project, document no. 275, 35b, Captain Nathaniel Butler, Letter to the Earl of Warwick, October 9, 1620.
179. The *White Lion*, although the source of the fourteen blacks referenced, did not bring them to Bermuda. They were exchanged at sea with a Captain Kerby who physically brought the fourteen Angolans to Bermuda. See Kingsbury, *Records of the Virginia Company*, 2:395. See also Tyler, *Narratives of Early Virginia*, 282 n1.
180. *Narratives of Early Virginia*, 282n1.
181. According to the Muster of 1624–1625, the woman by the name of Angelo was reported to have arrived in the colony on board the *Treasurer*, thereby being the said Angolan left in Virginia. Hotten, *Original Lists of Persons of Quality*, 201–65. See also Brown, *Genesis of the United States*, 885.

Chapter 6

182. FP, vol. 3, no. 3, Summer 1995, 168. See Thorndale, "Virginia Census of 1619," 60–168.
183. When the census was taken the terminology of "other Christians" was to mean white settlers in the colony, and the terminology of "Non-Christians" was intended to mean non-white inhabitants. It is unclear if it was known that the Angolans were in fact Catholic Christians or not, substantiating that the intent of the verbiage was to denote skin color and not necessarily religious affiliation. Thorndale, "Virginia Census of 1619," 60–168.
184. The March 1620 census did not provide the name of any of the inhabitants, including the Angolans. The year of the census has erroneously confounded some historians who believed that the census was taken in March 1619 and that there were thirty-two Africans already in the colony prior to the arrival of the *While Lion* and the *Treasurer*. This was advanced by William Thorndale, who belived that the Angolans were already in the colony when the *White Lion* arrived on August 25, 1619. However, after a careful review by historian Martha McCartney, it was determined that the 1619 date reflects the old Julian calendar that was in use at the time, making the actual date March 1620 and not March 1619, reflecting that the new year did not start until the spring of each year. Thorndale, "Virginia Census of 1619," 60–168. See also McCartney, "Early Census Reprised," 178–96.

185. McIlwaine, *Minutes of the Council*, 196.

186. Present-day historians continue to debate how to arrive at the number of thirty-two Angolans on the 1620 census. Some will suggest that the terminology of "twenty and odd" means twenty and any odd number. Some will contend that an initial fourteen were left by the *White Lion* on August 25, 1619, and when the *Treasurer* arrived and abruptly departed, it left behind one Angolan woman, and that another fourteen or so came back to Virginia on another ship or pinnace, bringing the number to thirty-two, as stated in the census. To date, there is no credible information that documents that the *White Lion* left fewer than twenty-eight or so Angolans in Virginia, and there is no evidence that documents that they arrived first in Bermuda and arrived later in Virginia with only fourteen or so Angolans. It should be noted however that Lyon Gardiner Tyler, in his *Narratives of Early Virginia, 1606–1625*, 282–287, states in a footnote (1): "This Dutch man-of-war is the one which in August, 1619, sold to the settlers at Jamestown the first Africans imported into this country.... On its way to Jamestown the Dutch of Flemish man-of-war touched at the Bermudas, where Kerby, the captain, presented fourteen negroes to Governor Kendal in return for supplies." There are no present-day primary source documents to substantiate this claim.

187. According to historian Wesley Frank Craven in *Dissolution of the Virginia Company: The Failure of a Colonial Experiment*, "It has often been assumed that Elfrith disposed of some of his [blacks] in Virginia, but there is no evidence to support this. He spent very little time there, not enough in fact to secure necessary supplies from the inhabitants of Kecoughtan [Point Comfort] who in their reception of him were anything but friendly, and had he disposed of any of his slaves they would certainly have been party in exchange for supplies. Moreover, he and the Captain of the *White Lion* evenly divided the sixty Angolans, netting him 30 captives. With the exception of the Angolan woman named Angelo who went to shore with the ship's officer and both were left behind, there is no mention of any [Angolans] other than those with the 29 he had when he arrived at Bermuda in September 1619. It seems certain, therefore, that the first slaves introduced into Virginia were not aboard the *Treasurer* but rather those of the *White Lion*." See Craven, *Dissolution of the Virginia Company*, 130–31. See also Kingsbury, *Records of the Virginia Company*, 2:402.

188. Craven, *Dissolution of the Virginia Company*, 131.

189. Lefroy, *Memorials of the Discovery*, 722. During the interrogatories in response to the allegations made by the Spanish Ambassador,

John Weston testified that the *Treasurer* "arrived in the Somer Islands in September 1619." See also Coldham, *Complete Book of Emigrants 1607–1660*, 181.

190. Report of the Royal Commission on Historic Manuscripts Public Records Office, Kew, England, courtesy of the LoV, Virginia Colonial Records Project, document no. 261, 35b, Captain Nathaniel Butler, Letter to the Earl of Warwick, October 9, 1620; John Dutton letter to the Earl of Warwick, January 20, 1620. If Dutton's account is accurate as to the number of Africans brought to Bermuda, less than the one African was left behind in Virginia, and that would be the woman recorded as Angelo, then known as Angela, in the Muster of 1624–1625. See Hotten, *Original Lists of Persons of Quality*, 201–65.

191. Report of the Royal Commission on Historic Manuscripts Public Records Office, Kew, England, courtesy of the LoV, Virginia Colonial Records Project, document no. 261. In the John Dutton letter to Lord Rich (Earl of Warwick), there are several technical errors that must be pointed out. The letter is dated January 20, 1619; this date is clearly an error, as neither the *Treasurer* nor the *Garland* arrived until the fall of 1619. The correct date on the letter should have been January 20, 162. Second, in the letter, Dutton states that the *Treasurer* arrived on October 20, 1619. However, he may have confused the date with the arrival of the other ship owned by Lord Rich, the *Warwick*, which arrived on the stated date. The *Treasurer* more than likely arrived in Bermuda mid-September, as testified by Richard Stafford at his June 3, 1620 deposition.

192. According to the Institute of Nautical Archaeology, the length of the ship was approximately 98 to 112 feet.

193. Lefroy, *Memorials of the Discovery*, 149. See also Kingsbury, *Records of the Virginia Company*, 3:282–83.

194. Lefroy, *Memorials of the Discovery*, 149. See also Kingsbury, *Records of the Virginia Company*, 3:282–83.

195. Institute of Nautical Archaeology, https://nauticalarch.org.

196. According to Keith Forbes, verified by the Institute of Nautical Archaeology, to the huge surprise of an excavation crew and "scientists several hundred years later, they dug up the *Warwick* and discovered she had been armed to the teeth, far too heavily armed for a mere supply ship. Her remains are still there, reburied in the sand. She was one of the newest and most technologically advanced ships of her era." See Keith Archibald Forbes, "Bermuda's History from 1500 to 1699: How It Is linked to Events in Europe, the United States of America,

United Kingdom and Canada," www.bermuda-online.org. The finding of the *Warwick* is certainly a historic milestone but may contradict a letter written by Governor Butler to his engineer on June 24, 1622, in which he states, "To my Loving Friend Jacobb the Ship-Carpenter at Sommerseate: You are my engineer…the first thing you must do, must be fitting of these two crazy boats. When you have done what you can there, fail not to come up to town, and you shall have the help of my [blacks], and the whole gang, to break up the *Treasurer*, and to get your iron work there. Bring up with you also your ensign, for we will try what we may be further done with the *Warwick*, and will scorne to leave any good work behind us in these kinds undone. Forgett not also to bring your tools for you know our boats are to be repaired, and oars are to be made for the new boat, before the time runs away." See also Lefroy, *Memorials of the Discovery*, 252.

197. Coldham, *English Adventurers and Emigrants*, 1:150. See also Kingsbury, *Records of the Virginia Company*, 3:621.

198. Lefroy, *Memorials of the Discovery*, 157.

199. Report of the Royal Commission on Historic Manuscripts Public Records Office, Kew, England, courtesy of the LoV, Virginia Colonial Records Project, document no. 275, Letter to the Earl of Warwick, October 9, 1620.

200. Tyler, *Narratives of Early Virginia*, 282n1.

201. John Wood testimony in examinations of allegations by the Spanish ambassador on June 3, 1620. High Court of the Admitalty (HCA), National Archives, Kew, England. See McCartney, "New Light on Virginia's First Africans," 19.

202. Hashaw, *Birth of Black America*, 300 n130.

203. Hotten, *Original Lists of Persons of Quality*, 244.

204. Bridenbaugh, *Jamestown*, 22.

205. Kingsbury, *Records of the Virginia Company*, 565–71. See also Bridenbaugh, *Jamestown*, 29.

206. Dorman, *Adventurers of Purse and Person*, 3.

207. "A Declaration of the State of the Colony and Affairs of Virginia… and a Relation of the Barbarous Massacre." See Kingsbury, *Records of the Virginia Company*, 3:541–612.

208. Matthew and Harrison, *Oxford Dictionary of National Biography*, 57: 551.

209. Craven, *Virginia Company of London*, 11n12; Campbell, *History of the Colony*, 169.

210. Robinson, *Mother Earth*, 27.

211. Based on ship manifests and colonial headrights, it appears that approximately 230 inhabitants in the colony may not have been properly included in the 1624 census when compared to the following census taken.

212. Ballagh, *History of Slavery in Virginia*, 29–30.

213. Thornton, "African-American Naming Patterns," 729.

214. Ibid.

215. Ibid, 739.

216. The Muster of 1624–1625 as well as the List of 1623 underreported a number of English and Angolans. The Muster did not count the English inhabitants at Captain William Ewen's plantation, including the four Angolans, John Gowen, Michael and Kathryn Blizzard, and Matthew who last name and full identify is unknown. See Hotten, *Original Lists of Persons of Quality*, 201–65.

217. The 1620 Census lists thirty-two Angolans in the colony. The preponderance of evidence would suggest that after the Powhatan's Massacre of 1622, several of the Angolans were slain, or they were taken or voluntarily left with their captives. This is supported by the 1646 treaty in which the Native Americans agreed to return all English and African captives, and any guns and Indian servants that they were detaining. Thorndale, "Virginia Census of 1619," 60–168. See also Hening, *Statutes at Large*, 1:325.

218. Hotten, *Original Lists of Persons of Quality*, 244.

Chapter 7

219. Fisher and Kelley, *Bound Away*, 28.

220. Ibid.

221. Morgan, "Headrights and Head Counts," 362.

222. Finkelman, *Encyclopedia of African American History*, 192–97.

223. Coldham, *Emigrants in Chains*, 41.

224. Ibid., 7.

225. Finkelman *Encyclopedia of African American History*, 192–97.

226. Hening, *Statutes at Large*, 1:257.

227. Fisher and Kelley, *Bound Away*, 28.

228. Morgan, "Headrights and Head Counts," 407.

229. Hening, *Statutes at Large*, 1:146.

230. Nugent, *Cavaliers and Pioneers*, 118.

231. Each of the original eight shires has been renamed, and for research purposes, county files are found under the

present-day name of the revised county name: Accomac Shire (now Northampton and Accomack Counties), Charles City Shire (now Charles City County), Charles River Shire (York County), Elizabeth City Shire (consolidated with the City of Hampton), Henrico Shire (Henrico County), James City Shire (James City County), Warwick River Shire (consolidated with the City of Newport News) and Warrosquyoake Shire (Isle of Wight County).

232. The Deeds, Orders and Will books can be found in each of the original eight shires/counties. Over the years, some of the earliest colonial records may have been destroyed by water, fire or war; therefore, there may be a gap in some of the records.

233. Berlin, *Many Thousands Gone*, 42–43.

Epilogue

234. On July 4, 1776, the former British colonies announced through the Declaration of Independence their independence of British rule. The declaration provided the British monarch and Parliament the specific reasons for proclaiming independence, including the statement: "We hold these truths to be self-evident, that all men are created equal, that they are endowed by their Creator with certain unalienable Rights, that among these are Life, Liberty and the pursuit of Happiness." However, the declarative statement was meant to mean and interpreted that only "white men are created equal." In order to defend the statement and the institution of slavery, the term or phrase "peculiar institution," was used, a euphemism often used by legislative bodies, particularly in the South, to defend the institution without contradicting the purpose and the intent of the phrase in the Declaration that "all men are created equal."

235. Indentures had set time limits for adults. As the law changed from time to time, the term of the indenture slightly fluctuated. For children, the indentures also fluctuated from the age of maturity, whatever they might have been at the time, and for other minor children until the age of thirty or so years, according to written indentures and court cases.

236. Ackroyd, *Foundation*, 42–43.

237. Ibid., 105.

238. Davies, *Isles*, 470–75.

239. Morgan, *Oxford Illustrated History of Britain*, 288.

240. Ibid., 286

241. Ibid., 289–90.

242. Ibid., 288.

243. Keegan, "Can You Make A Non-Racist Tarzan Movie?"

244. Hashaw, *Birth of Black America*, 15.

245. Echeverria-Estrada and Batalova, "Sub-Saharan African Immigrants in the United States."

246. Virginia's hot summers and relatively mild winters, along with moderate rainfall throughout the year, classify the state's climate as subtropical temperate.

247. Davies, *Isles*, 788.

248. In the Muster of 1624–1625, twenty-three Angolans can be found. As with the English laborers with whom they worked and lived with, the Angolans were listed with the legal status of "servant" next to their names. See Hotten, *Original Lists of Persons of Quality*, 201–65. See also Jester and Woodroof, *Adventurers of Purse and Person*. See also Dorman, *Adventures of Purse and Person*, 2004.

249. Hening, *Statutes at Large*, 2:170.

250. In 1498, Christopher Columbus, having stopped at the Canary and Cape Verde Islands, began to import and introduce Africans to the West Indies and Saint Augustine in what became Spanish Florida. In 1586, Africans were part of a Spanish expedition that settled an outpost in what is present-day South Carolina.

251. Sluiter, "New Light," 396–97.

252. Hotten, *Original Lists of Persons of Quality*, 169–89. See also Jester and Woodroof, *Adventurers of Purse and Person*; Dorman, *Adventurers of Purse and Person*.

253. Voyages database. The total number of 305,326 African enslaved reflects current data on the actual number leaving the shores of Africa and arriving in English North America/the United States of America. Some historians use a slightly higher number, between 305,326 and 380,000, which reflects the inclusion of enslaved brought to the shores of English North America/the United States of America from the Caribbean islands—these were often known as "seasoned slaves."

BIBLIOGRAPHY

Primary Sources

Barbour, Philip L., ed. *The Jamestown Voyages, Under the First Charter, 1606–1609*. 2 vols. Cambridge, UK: Cambridge University Press, 1696.

Battell, Andrew. *The Strange Adventures of Andrew Battel of Leigh, in Angola and the Adjoining Regions*. Reprinted from *Purchas His Pilgrimes* (London, 1625), edited by E.G. Ravenstein. London: Hakluyt Society, 1905.

Coldham, Peter Wilson. *The Complete Book of Emigrants 1607–1660: A Comprehensive Listing Compiled from English Public Records of Those Who Took Ship to the Americas for Political, Religious, and Economic Reasons; of Those Who Were Deported for Vagrancy, Roguery, or Non-Conformity; and of Those Who Were Sold to Labour in the New Colonies, English Adventurers and Emigrants, 1609–1660: Abstracts of Examinations in the High Court of Admiralty with Reference to Colonial America*. Baltimore: Genealogical Publishing, 1987.

———. *Emigrants in Chains: A Social History of Forced Emigration to the Americas of Felons, Destitute Children, Political and Religious Non-Conformists, Vagabonds, Beggars and other Undesirables, 1607–1776*. Baltimore: Genealogical Publishing, 1992.

———. *English Adventurers and Emigrants, 1609–1660: Abstracts of Examinations in the High Court of Admiralty with Reference to Colonial America*. Baltimore: Clearfield Company Reprints & Reminders, 1984.

Dorman, John Fredrick. *Adventurers of Purse and Person*. Baltimore: Genealogical Publishing, 2004.

Ferrar, Nicholas, D.R. Ransome and J.E.B. Mayor. *Ferrar Papers, 1559-1620-1637*. Cambridge, UK: Cambridge University Press, n.d.

Haile, Edward Wright, ed. *Jamestown Narratives: Eyewitness Accounts of the Virginia Colony, the First Decade, 1607–1617*. Champlain, VA: RoundHouse Press, 1988.

Hening, William W., ed. *The Statutes at Large; Being a Collection of All Laws of Virginia, from the First Session of the Legislature in the Year 1619 [to 1792]*. 13 vols. New York and Philadelphia, 1819–1823.

Hotten, John Camden. *Original Lists of Persons of Quality: Emigrants, Religious Exiles, Political Rebels, Serving Men Sold for a Term of Years, Apprentices, Children Stolen, Maidens Pressed, and Others Who Went from Great Britain to the American Plantations, 1600–1700*. From the MSS, State Paper Department of Her Majesty's Public Record Office, London, England, 1874. Reprint, Baltimore: Genealogical Publishing, 1986.

Jester, Annie Lash, and Martha Woodroof. *Adventurers of Purse and Person Virginia, 1607–1625*. Baltimore: Genealogical Publishing, 1956.

Kingsbury, Susan Myra, ed. *The Records of the Virginia Company of London*. 4 vols. Washington, D.C.: Government Printing Office, 1906–1935.

McIlwaine, Henry Read, ed. *Legislative Journals of the Council of Colonial Virginia, 1619–1776*. Richmond, VA: Colonial Press, 1918–1919.

————. *Minutes of the Council and General Court of Colonial Virginia, 1622–1632, 1670–1676*, Richmond, VA: Colonial Press, 1925.

McIlwaine, Henry Read, and W.L. Hall. *Executive Journals of the Council of Colonial Virginia*. Richmond, VA: Virginia State Library, 1925.

Neill, Edward D. *Virginia Carolorum: The Colony Under the Rule of Charles the First and Second*. Albany, NY: J. Munsell's & Sons, 1886.

Nugent, Nell Marion. *Cavaliers and Pioneers: Abstracts of Virginia Land Patents and Grants, 1623–1800*. Richmond, VA: Dietz Printing, 1934.

Report Commission on Historic Manuscripts, Kew, England. Document No. 261, courtesy of the LoV, Virginia Colonial Records Project. John Dutton to the Earl of Warwick, January 20, 1620.

————. Document No. 261 35b, courtesy of the LoV, Virginia Colonial Records Project. John Dutton to the Earl of Warwick, January 20, 1620.

————. Document No. 275, courtesy of the LoV, Virginia Colonial Records Project. Letter to the Earl of Warwick, October 9, 1620.

Secondary Sources

Ackroyd, Peter. *Foundation: The History of England from Its Earliest Beginnings to the Tudors*. New York: Thomas Dunne Books, 2011.

Anderson, David, and Richard Rachbone, eds. *Africa's Urban Past*. London: Heinemann Publishers, 2000.

Appiah, Kwame Anthony, and Henry Louis Gates, eds. *Africana: The Encyclopedia of the African and African American Experience*. 2nd ed. New York: Oxford University Press, 2005.

Arber, Edward. *Travels and Works of Captain John Smith: President of Virginia and Admiral of New England, 1580–1631*. Edinburgh: John Grant, 1910.

Axtell, James. *After Columbus: Essays in the Ethnohistory of Colonial North America*. New York: Oxford University Press, 1988.

———. *The Rise and Fall of the Powhatan Empire: Indians in Seventeenth-Century Virginia*. Williamsburg, VA: Colonial Williamsburg Foundation, 1995.

Ballagh, James Curtis. *A History of Slavery in Virginia*. Baltimore: Johns Hopkins Press, 1902.

Bemiss, Samuel M. *The Three Charters of the Virginia Company of London*. Williamsburg: Virginia 350th Anniversary Celebration Corporation, 1957.

Berlin, Ira. *Generations of Captivity: A History of African-American Slaves*. Cambridge, MA: Belknap Press, 2003.

———. *Many Thousands Gone: The First Two Centuries of Slavery in North America*. Cambridge, MA: Harvard University Press, 1998.

Billings, Warren, ed. *The Papers of Sir William Berkeley, 1605–1677*. Richmond: Library of Virginia, 2007.

Blumrosen, Alfred W., and Ruth G. Blumrosen. *Slave Nation: How Slavery United the Colonies and Sparked the American Revolution*. Naperville, IL: Sourcebooks, 2005.

Boxer, Charles Ralph. *The Christian Century in Japan, 1549–1650*. Berkeley: University of California Press, 1951.

Brasio, Antonio. *Monumenta Missionaria Africana*. 15 vols. Lisboa: Agência Geral do Ultramar, Divisão de Publicações e Biblioteca, 1958–.

Bridenbaugh, Carl. *Jamestown: 1544–1699*. New York: Oxford University Press, 1980.

Brown, Alexander. *The First Republic in America: An Account of the Origin of This Nation, Written from the Records Then (1624) Concealed by the Council, Rather Than from the Histories Then Licensed by the Crown*. Boston: Houghton, Mifflin and Company, 1898.

————. *The Genesis of the United States: A Narrative of the Movement in England, 1605–1616, Which Resulted in the Plantation of North America by Englishmen, Disclosing the Contest Between England and Spain for the Possession of the Soil Now Occupied by the United States of America; Set Forth*. Boston: Houghton, Mifflin and Company, 1898.

Bruce, Philip Alexandria. *Economic History of Virginia in the Seventeenth Century: An Inquiry into the Material Condition of the People, Based upon Original and Contemporaneous Records*. New York: MacMillan and Company, 1896.

————. *Virginia: Rebirth of the Old Dominion*. New York: Lewis Publishing, 1929.

Cadornega, Antonio de Oliveria de. *Historia Geral Das Guerras Anglomas (1680–81)* (1940–1942) ed. Jose Matias Delgado and Manuel Alves de Cunha. 3 vols. Lisbon: 1972. In Portugese.

Campbell, Charles. *History of the Colony and Ancient Dominion of Virginia*. Philadelphia: N.p., 1860.

Cannon, John. *Dictionary of British History*. New York: Oxford University Press, 2001.

Cawthorne, Nigel. *Kings and Queens of England, From the Saxon Kings to the House of Windsor*. London: Arcturus Publishing, 2009.

Churchill, Winston S. *The Birth of Britain, A History of Speaking Peoples*. Vol. 1. New York: Dodd, Mead & and Company, 1956.

Craven, Wesley Frank. *Dissolution of the Virginia Company: The Failure of a Colonial Experiment*. New York: Oxford University Press, 1932.

————. *The Virginia Company of London, 1606–1624*. Williamsburg: Virginia 350th Anniversary Celebration Corporation, 1957.

Davies, Norman. *The Isles, A History*. New York: Oxford University Press, 1999.

De Villiers, Marq, and Shelia Hirtle. *Into Africa: A Journey through Ancient Empires*. Toronto: Key Porter Books, 1997.

Diop, Cheikh Anta. *Precolonial Black Africa: A Comparative Study of the Political and Social Systems of Europe and Black Africa, from Antiquity to the Formation of Modern States*. Brooklyn, NY: Lawrence Hill Books, 1987.

Egerton, Douglas R. *Death or Liberty: African Americans and Revolutionary America*. New York: Oxford University Press, 2009.

Eltis, Davis, and David Richardson. *Atlas of the Trans-Atlantic Slave Trade*. New Haven, CT: Yale University Press, 2010.

Faria, Manuel Severim da. "Historia Portugueza e de utras Provinicias do Occidente desde o Anno de 1610 de 1640...." Biblioteca Nacional de Lisboa, Lisboa, Portugal. In Portuguese.

Finkelman, Paul, ed. *Encyclopedia of African American History, 1619–1895: From the Colonial Period to the Age of Frederick Douglass*. New York: Oxford University Press, 2006.

Fisher, David Hackett, and James C. Kelley. *Bound Away: Virginia in the Westward Movement*. Charlottesville: University of Virginia Press, 2000.

Glover, Lorri, and Daniel Blake Smith. *The Shipwreck that Saved Jamestown: The Sea Venture Castaways and the Fate of America*. New York: Henry Holt and Company, 2008.

Hashaw, Tim. *The Birth of Black America, the First African Americans and the Pursuit of Freedom at Jamestown*. New York: Carroll and Graf Publishers, 2007.

Hatch, Charles E. *The First Seventeen Years, Virginia, 1607–1624*: Williamsburg: Virginia 350th Anniversary Celebration Commission, 1957.

Heinegg, Paul. *Free African Americans of North Carolina, Virginia and South Carolina from the Colonial Period to about 1820*. 2 vols. 5th ed. Baltimore: Clearfield, 2008.

Heintze, Beatrix, *Das Ende des Unabhangigen Staats Ndongo (Angola): Neue Chronologie und Reinterpretation* (1617–1630). Studien zur Geschichte Angolas, Lisboa, Portugal. In Portuguese.

Hock, James A., *When Ancestors Weep: Healing the Soul from Intergenerational Trauma*. Bloomington, IN: Abbott Press, 2018.

Jester, Annie Lash. *Domestic Life in Virginia in the Seventeenth Century*. Williamsburg: Virginia 350th Anniversary Celebration Commission, 1957.

Kendi, Ibram X. *Stamped from the Beginning: The Definitive History of Racist Ideas in America*. New York: Nation Books, 2016.

Knight, K.I. *Unveiled, The Twenty and Odd: Documenting the First Africans in England's America, 1619–1625 and Beyond*. Florida: First Freedom Publishing, 2019.

Lefroy, J.H. *Memorials of the Discovery and Early Settlement of the Bermudas or Somers Islands, 1515–1685*. Hamilton: Bermuda Government Library, 1932.

Mann, Kenny. *African Kingdoms of the Past, Kongo, Ndongo, West Central Africa*. Parsippany, NJ: Dillon Press, 1996.

Marshal, St. Julien Ravenel, ed. *The Jamestown Century: A Collection of Essays*. Alexandria, VA: Washington and Northern Virginia Company, 2010.

Matthew, H.C.G., and Brian Harrison. *Oxford Dictionary of National Biography, From the Earliest Times to the Year 2000*. Vol. 57. New York: Oxford University Press, n.d.

McCartney, Martha. *Jamestown People to 1800: Landowners, Public Officials, Minorities, and Native Leaders*. Baltimore: Genealogical Publishing, 2012.

———. *Virginia Immigrants and Adventurers 1607–1635: A Biographical Dictionary*. Baltimore: Genealogical Publishing, 2007.

McCary, Ben C. *Indians in Seventeenth-Century Virginia*. Williamsburg: Virginia 350th Anniversary Celebration Commission, 1957.

McMillan, Hamilton. *Sir Walter Raleigh's Lost Colony*. Raleigh, NC: Edwards & Broughton Printing, 1907.

Meacham, Jon. *Thomas Jefferson: The Art of Power*. New York: Random House, 2012.

Montecucculo, Giovanni Antonio Cavazzi da. "Missions Evangelica al regno de Congo" MSS Araldi (ca 1668), V.A: Book 26, Lisboa, Portugal. English translation.

Morgan, Edmund S. *American Slavery American Freedom: The Ordeal of Colonial Virginia*. New York: W.W. Norton and Company, 1975.

Morgan, Kenneth O., ed. *The Oxford Illustrated History of Britain*. New York: Oxford University Press, 1984.

Mossiker, Frances. *Pocahontas, The Life and the Legend*. New York: Da Capo Press, 1996.

Murphy, Ric. *Freedom Road: An American Family Saga from Jamestown to World War*. 2nd ed. Alexandria, VA: Franklin Pearson Publishers, 2014.

Murphy, Ric, and Timothy Stephens. *Section 27 and Freedman's Village in Arlington National Cemetery: The African American History of America's Most Hallowed Ground*. Jefferson, NC: McFarland Publishers, 2019.

Neill, Edward D. *History of the Virginia Company of London*. 2nd ed. New York: Burt Franklin, 1968.

Niane, D.T., ed. *Africa from the Twelfth to the Sixteenth Century*. London: Heinemann, 1984.

Nichols, Roger L. *Indians in the United States, A Comparative History*. Lincoln: University of Nebraska Press, 1998.

Parent, Anthony S. *Foul Means: The Formation of a Slave Society in Virginia, 1660–1740*. Chapel Hill: University of North Carolina Press, 2003.

Phillips, Jonathan. *Holy Warriors: A Modern History of the Crusades*. New York: Random House, 2009.

Phillips, Richard Hayes. *Without Indentures: Index to White Slave Children in Colonial Court Records (Maryland and Virginia)*. Baltimore: Genealogical Publishing, 2013.

Pickett, Margaret F., and Dwayne W. Pickett. *The European Struggle to Settle North America: Colonizing Attempts by England, France and Spain, 1521–1608*. Jefferson, NC: McFarland and Company, 2011.

Randall, Willard Sterne. *Thomas Jefferson: A Life*. New York: Henry Holt and Company, 1993.

Rice, James D. *Tales from a Revolution: Bacon's Rebellion in the Transformation of Early America*. New York Oxford University Press, 2012.

Robinson, W. Stitt. *Mother Earth: Land Grants in Virginia, 1607–1699*. Williamsburg: Virginia 350th Anniversary Celebration Commission, 1957.

Rouse, A.L. *Sir Walter Ralegh: His Family and His Private Life*. New York: Harper and Brothers, 1962.

Russell, John Henderson. *The Free Negro in Virginia, 1619–1865*. Reprint. New York: Negro Universities Press, 1969.

Schmidt, Ethan A. *The Divided Dominion: Social Conflict and Indian Hatred in Early Virginia*. Boulder: University Press of Colorado, 2015.

Shillington, Kevin. *History of Africa*. Oxford, Malaysia: Macmillan Publishers, 2012.

Soares, Bishop Manuel Baptista. "Copia Dos Excessos." September 7, 1619 in Brasio, ed., *Monumenta Missionaria Africana*, vol. 4. In Portugese.

Stevenson, J. Court, and Karen Sundberg. *Historical Shoreline Configurations at Cove Point from Original Patents and Later Shoreline Surveys*. Lusby, MD: Cove Point Natural Heritage Trust, 1997.

Taylor, Alan. *American Colonies*. New York: Viking Books, 2001.

Thomas, Hugh. *The Story of the Atlantic Slave Trade: 1440–1870*. New York: Simon and Schuster, 1997.

Thornton, John K. *Warfare in Atlantic Africa, 1500–1800*. London: University College, 1999.

Tolan, John, Gilles Veinstein and Henry Laurens. *Europe and the Islamic World, A History*. Princeton, NJ: Princeton University Press, 2013.

Trevelyan, Raleigh. *Sir Walter Raleigh*. New York: Henry Holt and Company, 2002.

Turman, Nora Miller. *George Yeardley: Governor of Virginia and Organizer of the General Assembly in 1619*. Richmond, VA: Garrett and Massie, 1959.

Tyler, Lyon Gardiner. *Narratives of Early Virginia, 1616–1625*. New York: Charles Scribner's Sons, 1907.

U.S. Department of Commerce, Census Bureau. 1790 Census, Census of Population and Housing.

Van Reybrouck, David. *Congo: The Epic History of a People*. New York: Harper Collins, 2014.

Vasconcellos, Luis Mendes des. "Adbierre de las Cosas de que Tiene Falta el Gouierno de Angola." (1616). In Brasio, ed., *Monumenta Missionaria Africana*, vol. 5. In Portugese.

Wallenfeldt, Jeff, ed. *Africa to America: From the Middle Passage Through the 1930s*. New York: Britannica Educational Publishing, 2011.

Washburn, Wilcomb E. *Virginia Under Charles I and Cromwell, 1625–1660.* Williamsburg: Virginia 350th Anniversary Celebration Commission, 1957.

Williams, Tony. *The Jamestown Experiment: The Remarkable Story of the Enterprising Colony and the Unexpected Results That Shaped America.* Naperville, IL: Sourcebooks, 2011.

Wise, Jennings Cropper. *Ye Kingdome of Accawmacke: Or the Eastern Shore of Virginia in the Seventeenth Century.* Richmond, VA: Bell Book and Stationery Company, 1911.

Wood, Betty. *The Origins of American Slavery, Freedom and Bondage in the English Colonies.* New York: Hill and Wang, 1997.

Woodward, Grace Steele. *Pocahontas.* Norman: University of Oklahoma Press, 1969.

Woolley, Benjamin. *Savage Kingdom: The True Story of Jamestown, 1607, and the Settlement of America.* New York: Harper Collins, 2007.

Journals, Magazines and Newspapers

"Bacon's Rebellion, William Sherwood's Account." *Virginia Magazine of History and Biography*, vol. 1, 1893. Alexandria Public Library.

Brown, B. Bernard. "The Battle of the Severn: Its Antecedents and Consequences, 1651–1655." *Maryland Historical Magazine*, vol. 14, 1919.

Coldham, Peter Wilson. "The Voyage of the *Neptune* to Virginia, 1618–1619, and the Disposition of Its Cargo." *Virginia Magazine of History and Biography*, vol. 87, January 1979.

Dawsey, Josh. "Trump Derides Protections for Immigrants from 'Shithole' Counties." *Washington Post*, January 12, 2018.

Handlin, Oscar, and Mary F. Handlin. "Origins of the Southern Labor System." *William and Mary Quarterly* 7, no. 3 (January 1950).

Journal of House of Burgesses, October 1666. Virginia Historical Society, *Virginia Magazine of History and Biography* 17, n.d.

Keegan, Rebecca. "Can You Make A Non-Racist Tarzan Movie?" *Los Angeles Times.* July 1, 2016. "Management of Slaves, 1672." *Virginia Magazine of History and Biography*, vol. 7, June 1900.

McCartney, Martha. "An Early Census Reprised." *Quarterly Bulletin of the Archeological Society of Virginia* 54 (1999).

———. "New Light on Virginia's First Africans." *Archeological Society of Virginia, Quarterly Bulletin* 74, no. 1 (March 2019).

Morgan, Edmund S. "Headrights and Head Counts: A Review Article." *Virginia Magazine of History and Biography*, vol. 80, 1972.

Rodrigues, Pero. "Historia da Resdencia Dos Padres da Companhia de Jesus em Angola, e Cousas Tocantes ao Reino, e Conquista" (May 1, 1594). In Brasio, ed., *Monumenta Missionaria Africana*. In Portugese.

Simmons, Ann M. "African Immigrants Are More Educated than Most—Including People Born in the U.S." *Lose Angeles Times*, January 12, 2018.

Sluiter, Engel. "New Light on the '20 and Odd' Africans Arriving in Virginia in 1619." *William and Mary Quarterly* 54, no. 2 (April 1997).

Thorndale, William. "The Virginia Census of 1619." *Magazine of Virginia Genealogy* 33, no. 3 (Summer 1995).

Thornton, John. "African-American Naming Patterns." *William and Mary Quarterly* 50, no. 4 (October 1993).

———. "The African Experience of the '20 and Odd' Africans Arriving in Virginia in 1619." *William and Mary Quarterly* 55, no. 3 (July 1998).

———. "Legitimacy and Political Power: Queen Njinga, 1624–1663." *Journal of African History* 32 (1991).

Electronic Sources

Echeverria-Estrada, Carlos, and Jeanne Batalova. "Sub-Saharan African Immigrants in the United States." Migration Policy Institute, November 6, 2019. www.migrationpolicy.org.

Emory University. "Voyages: The Trans-Atlantic Slave Trade Database." http://slavevoyages.org.

Institute of Nautical Archaeology, "*Warwick* Research Project." nauticalarch.org.

Unam Sanctum Catholicam. "Dum Diversas (English Translation)." February 5, 2011. unamsanctamcatholicam.blogspot.com.

INDEX

ABOUT THE AUTHOR

R ic Murphy is national vice president for history for the Afro-American Historical and Genealogical Society. As an acclaimed historian, scholar and lecturer, he has presented throughout North America, Europe and Africa. An award-winning author, he explores the rich contributions made by African Americans in U.S. history. His family dates to the earliest colonial periods of Plymouth, Massachusetts, and of Jamestown, Virginia. Murphy's lineage has been evaluated and accepted by several heredity societies, including the Daughters of the American Revolution; the National Society of the Sons of Colonial New England; the Sons of the American Revolution; the Sons of the Union Veterans of the Civil War; and the Sons and Daughters of the United States Middle Passage. Murphy was a fellow at Harvard University, Kennedy School; he earned a master's degree from Boston University and bachelor's from the University of Massachusetts.

Visit us at
www.historypress.com
....